CULTURE SMART!
GREECE

Constantine Buhayer

·K·U·P·E·R·A·R·D·

First published in Great Britain 2005
by Kuperard, an imprint of Bravo Ltd
59 Hutton Grove, London N12 8DS
Tel: +44 (0) 20 8446 2440   Fax: +44 (0) 20 8446 2441
www.culturesmartguides.com
Inquiries: sales@kuperard.co.uk

Culture Smart! is a registered trademark of Bravo Ltd

Distributed in the United States and Canada
by Random House Distribution Services
1745 Broadway, New York, NY 10019
Tel: +1 (212) 572-2844   Fax: +1 (212) 572-4961
Inquiries: csorders@randomhouse.com

Series Editor Geoffrey Chesler
Design Bobby Birchall

ISBN 978 1 85733 369 5

British Library Cataloguing in Publication Data
A CIP catalogue entry for this book is available from the
British Library

Printed in Malaysia

Cover image: Whitewashed church, Santorini.
Travel Ink/Roger Rowland

About the Author

CONSTANTINE BUHAYER is a London Greek who supervises for the International Liaison and Communication MA program at the University of Westminster, London, and lectures on bilingual translation. He is also a country analyst on Greece and Cyprus for *Jane's Sentinel*, has reported on Greece and Europe for the BBC, and in 2004 contributed to the coverage of the Athens Olympics for the *New York Times*. Since 2001 he has been a regular Associate Producer on CBS news's *60 Minutes*. He is currently writing a book on the history and impact of the Greeks in Britain.

**The Culture Smart! series is continuing to expand.
For further information and latest titles visit**
www.culturesmartguides.com

The publishers would like to thank **CultureSmart!**Consulting for its help in researching and developing the concept for this series.

CultureSmart!Consulting creates tailor-made seminars and consultancy programs to meet a wide range of corporate, public-sector, and individual needs. Whether delivering courses on multicultural team building in the USA, preparing Chinese engineers for a posting in Europe, training call-center staff in India, or raising the awareness of police forces to the needs of diverse ethnic communities, it provides essential, practical, and powerful skills worldwide to an increasingly international workforce.

For details, visit www.culturesmartconsulting.com

CultureSmart!Consulting and **CultureSmart!** guides have both contributed to and featured regularly in the weekly travel program "Fast Track" on BBC World TV.

contents

contents

Map of Greece

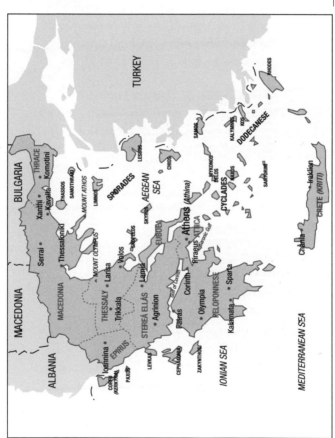

introduction

...Why so quiet? Look into your heart,
weren't you happy as we left Greece behind?
But what's the point of fooling ourselves?—
indeed, that wouldn't be properly Hellenic.

So let us admit the truth at last:
we, too, are Greek by culture—what else are we?—
but with tastes and feeling specific to our own country.
Tastes and feelings that sometimes seem strange
to the Hellenic values that shaped our world.

C. Cavafy, "Returning from Greece," 1901
(Adapted from the Greek by Constantine Buhayer)

Greece is an electrifying experience. When we
enter Greek space we are returning to the cradle
of humanity—or, at the very least, to the cradle
of its Western wing. This is where people
designed our society, with its political, ethical,
and scientific values. Since antiquity traders,
scholars, theologians, and all types of teachers
have traveled out of its lands to format,
formulate, and reformat the world. Thus it was
an Athenian scholar, Theodorus of Tarsus, who
in 669 CE arrived in southern Britain as
Archbishop of Canterbury and established a
Greek and Latin school to civilize the newly

arrived Germanic tribes. Most important,
he introduced an everlasting Greek
infrastructure, the parish system, which
parceled the land into fixed and manageable
civic units, centered upon a church.

In a way, part of us forever belongs to the
Hellenic world, and expectations are therefore
high, so you could be in for a shock if you find
yourself plunged into the living Greek reality.
Greece arouses passions, and today's visitor can
develop responses to the country that range from
unbridled fascination to vociferous objection. After
all, it is no exaggeration to say that entire nations
have been mobilized in the past for and against
the Greeks, some to wipe them out, others to join
their cause. Many chose to become "them."

Culture Smart! Greece sets out to equip
travelers with essential information about the
background, values, and attitudes of the people
they will meet, and practical guidelines on how to
understand and deal with unfamiliar situations.
Even the vital historical section concentrates on
relevant but unusual examples that say something
about today's Greeks. For those who connect with
the inner life of this gifted and important people,
there are riches aplenty.

Key Facts

Official Name	Hellenic Republic (*Ellinikí Demokratía*). Also called Greece, (*Elláda, Hellás*)	The inhabitants are called Greeks; also Hellenes. The Hellenic Republic Is a member of the EU and NATO.
Capital City	Athens (Athina)	Population, just under 5 million
Major Cities	Thessaloniki (second city); population around 1 million	Other cities include Heraklion, Larisa, and Patras, the 2006 cultural capital of Europe.
Area	50,949 sq. miles (131,958 sq. km)	Probably the most sea-oriented country in the world
Borders	Albania, FYRO Macedonia, Bulgaria, Turkey	
Climate	Variable, due to its crenellated terrain and long coastline. The mountainous north gets winter snow. The islands and central Greece are humid. The south has more gentle winters. Scorching summers are common across the land.	
Currency	Euro. Until recently the currency was the Drachma.	Most people relate the cost of living in Drachmas (1 Euro = 341 Drachmas).
Population	10,645,343, of whom 80% live in cities. Nearly half the population lives in Athens.	The last census excluded hundreds of thousands of recent legal and illegal immigrants.
Language	Greek	
Religion	Greek Orthodox Christianity	

Ethnic Makeup	98% of the native population is Greek.	Minorities mostly include Muslims, Pomaks, Gypsies, Slav Macedonians.
Government	Parliamentary Democracy headed by a President, based on the 1975 Constitution	
Media	The main newspapers are *Kathimeriní*, *Ta Néa*, *Eleftherotypía*, and *To Bíma*. The Greek news agency is ANA (with English and French services).	
Media: English Language	An English version of *Kathimerini* is distributed with the *International Herald Tribune*. *Athens News* is a weekly newspaper.	Hotels have satellite services. There are also Greek weeklies in French and German.
Video / TV	PAL system	
Electricity	230 volts, 50 Hz.	Two-prong continental plugs are used.
Telephone	The country code for Greece is 30. The city code for Athens is 201.	In Greece you need to dial the regional code, even within the same region. To dial out of Greece, dial 00 followed by the country code.
Time Zone	GMT+2 hours	Summertime and wintertime change with the rest of Europe.

chapter one

LAND &
PEOPLE

CONTRADICTIONS, CONTINUITIES, AND CONTRIBUTIONS

From the day of its emergence as a modern nation-state, Greece sailed against the wind and set many precedents. This theme will recur throughout the book. After debating its freedom for centuries, it came into existence by staging a revolution in 1821 to oust its Turkish Ottoman masters; soon it was fighting and arguing its way to independence. At the time, this stood out as a global and challenging precedent, because the world was being carved up between ever-growing empires—British, French, Russian, Dutch, or Austro-Hungarian. Greek independence set a "dangerous" precedent for other peoples and was a cause of friction between the big powers, most of whom wanted either to take the country over or to suppress it. But this was not, according to public European imagination, an ordinary people. These were the descendants of Homer, Aristotle, and Pericles. Europe was adopting the Greek style for its official architecture, while Romanticism animated the passions of the European intelligentsia and even the emerging "working classes." They wanted to see the Greeks succeed, and to restore the glory of their ancient civilization. All things Hellenic were in fashion, and the Greeks seemed unstoppable.

Therefore, by the time this European enthusiasm waned in the late 1830s the country had established its independence. In fact, Greeks began dreaming of reestablishing their own, Byzantine empire. Crucially, this was no venture to conquer distant peoples, but to unite their own people, spread from British-held Corfu to the far ends of the Pontus on the Black Sea (in today's northeastern Turkey), from Greek-dominated Wallachia (today's Romania) to Cyprus and Crete.

Meanwhile, opposite forces were hard at work. Not least, the great powers were against the rise of a strong, commercially enterprising nation in the East Mediterranean. In nineteenth-century northern Europe, misguided theories began emerging about "racial purity" and "superiority," and these doubted the linear links of the Greeks with their glorious ancestry. In the Balkan neighborhood, various peoples who were inspired by the feats of the nineteenth-century Hellenes began emulating them, then fighting them, and calling for their own nation-states.

Greece was moving toward a series of head-on collisions. Some of those experiences sharpened the country's survival skills, others generated new traumas. Today, you can see the human and cultural results of this interaction concentrated within the amazing natural beauty and urban sprawl that is modern Greece.

GEOGRAPHICAL OVERVIEW

The philosopher Aristotle (384–322 BCE) had already pointed out that his countrymen lived

around the Aegean Sea like frogs around a pond. The sea has always been associated with them. No Greek habitat is further than fifty miles from the convoluted shoreline that gives rise to an endless variety of natural bays, gulfs, inlets, lethal rock cliffs, and gentle beaches. Africa may cover nearly three hundred times the size of Greece; its coast is only three times longer. Greek territory is surrounded by three seas: the Aegean, the Ionian, and the Mediterranean. Across its pristine blue waters are scattered more than 3,000 islands, islets, and rock islands. The father of Western mysticism, George Gurdjieff, an early-twentieth-century Anatolian Greek, proposed that philosophical speculation was developed by those ancient Aegean fishermen, who, when stranded by the weather, would seek shelter in quiet places. To escape their boredom, he wrote, they played mental games, which the brighter ones developed into the Greek sciences that shaped humanity. Today, in those same sheltered recesses of the Aegean isles, people choose to relax, practice nudism, or read lengthy novels.

The mainland consists of interlaced mountain chains. Some of them descend abruptly into the sea, and may reappear in rows of islands. The terrain was difficult to cross and therefore ideal for the rise of the ancient independent city-states. Later, it sheltered Greek communities from invaders, offering vantage points for opening schools, and for fighting back. The physical features of the country and its unique archipelago forged a pronounced individuality and strong local patriotism. It was only in the 1990s that a comprehensive road network began linking the country, but even so, it remains an adventure to cross it east to west.

The largest plain is in Thessaly (central Greece), birthplace of the Centaurs, and stretching beneath Mount Olympus. Some islands, such as Crete, Corfu, or Chios, are large enough or in such strategic geopolitical locations to have sustained what might be labeled as a near-autonomous Hellenic civilization.

Climate

Greece has a Mediterranean climate. The further south you go, the warmer it gets. The best times are from May to mid June, and from September to late October, with temperatures in the range of 68–82°F (20–28°C). Summers are hot, normally over 90°F (32°C). Occasionally, a northern summer breeze, called *meltémi*, brings the temperature down to a bearable level. Winter months can see temperatures fall below 50°F (10°C), especially in northern Greece. Some of the islands experience great humidity. Macedonia, Epirus, and Thrace often have snow and mist in the winter. The Ionian Islands enjoy a wetter climate.

HELLENIC REPUBLIC OR GREECE?

Which is the proper name for Greece? Most of us are familiar with both terms. Aristotle observed that near Dodoni, in the northern province of Epirus, the Hellenes were referred to by their neighbors as *Grekoi*. The latter term was adopted (some would say pejoratively) by the Romans; it was popularized after Christianization. Another theory is that a Hellenic tribe moved to Sicily. Asked where they had originated from, they said Graia, their small city in Boeotia; hence, later, the Romans adopted the name *Graeci*. There are other theories, too.

Today, the official name of the country is the Hellenic Republic, or *Elliniki Dimokratia*. The people, in their own language call themselves *Hellenes*, and the country *Hellas* and *Ellada*. In EU documents, the acronym EL refers to *Elliniká*, or Greek (EN is for English, FR for French, DE for German, etc.). The references involving the term "Greek" are more usual. In maps and international organizations (including the EU, NATO, and the UN) the country is mentioned as Greece. At sporting events we see the acronym GRE. Car registrations are GR. The Internet addresses registered in Greece are indicated by ".gr" (for Canada, it is .ca; for America, .us; Italy, .it; etc.).

There is one more name. Arabic and most Muslim countries refer to the country as "Yunan." This even appears in the Hebrew Bible, in Genesis 10.1–4, where the Table of Nations lists the descendants of Noah and the nations they founded. One of Noah's grandsons was Yavan—a name associated with or derived from the word "Ionia," the ancient Greek province of Asia Minor. Appropriately enough, since these developments occurred after the great flood, Yavan sired the maritime peoples: his son Kittim gave rise to the Cypriots, and another son, Dodanim, to the people of Rhodes. Yavan's uncle Shem produced the more landbound Semitic peoples.

Today's Greece is a modernizing European country. In fact, this is the Third Hellenic Republic, which emerged in 1974, after the collapse of the short-lived junta regime.

MORE THAN JUST A LANGUAGE

WRATH, SING, GODDESS

Can one judge a people from its first recorded utterance? The opening words of the *Iliad* are "wrath," "sing," and "goddess." They make up the sentence "Μῆνιν ἄειδε, θεά, Πηληιάδεω ᾿Αχιλῆος" (*Menin aeide, thea, Peleiadeo Achileos*), or "Sing, goddess, of the wrath of Achilles, son of Peleus."

Homer's epic poem reflects an even older oral tradition. It depicts the tragedy and poignancy of friendship and family destroyed by battle. The cause of war was *érotas* (erotic love), or the abduction of the beautiful Helen by the handsome Trojan prince Paris. The main subject of the poem is the wrath of Achilles after his friend Patroclus was killed in battle. Certainly the Greeks can display a quick temper; you will not fail to catch their rich and vibrant musical tradition; and they have always appreciated physical beauty.

There is an extraordinary depth to the Greek language. It is not just the backbone of the people's recorded history; there are different dimensions to it. Each period of Hellenic civilization had its own communication needs, and would naturally update the language accordingly, but without discarding the earlier versions. To give a rough illustration, if this had happened to English (which only became an official language in 1362), British and American people would be speaking (or hearing) Anglo-Saxon, French, Chaucerian, Elizabethan, and American English, all used for different purposes.

In Greek, up to six different versions have survived. Occasionally, these versions of the language competed to the point of bloodshed. Entire regimes were undermined on linguistic grounds as different strands of society tried to impose their choices. And what were the choices? Well, after excluding the regional dialects, the official languages of Greek can be divided into Attic, Alexandrine/Ecclesiastic, *Katharévousa* (or purified), and *Koiné* (or Demotic) whose direct roots are in the Alexandrine.

Today, we have the Demotic as the state language—that is the one you will be communicating in with your friends, partners, and government institutions. Ecclesiastic Greek is that of the Church, while Attic Greek is an obligatory subject at schools, and also a university subject around the world.

The wonder is, how can grammar and vocabulary cause such upheavals? The answer is that Greek has been used to express domestic, administrative, legislative, theological, literary, security, or commercial concerns on a daily level for four thousand years. The language in which an olive farmer from Corfu will speak to his child today descends directly from that of Homer. Naturally, words that have been used and developed over thousands of years end up as a sort of ark—not just of animal life but also of human experiences and emotions. Each codified strand of the language has its own points of reference, its own moral and political priorities. It is as if each linguistic strand contains its own ideological variation.

The outcome of this is an amazing literary output; it also resulted in riots. In 1901 we have the "*Evangelakia*" riots over translations of the Bible into Demotic Greek. Between the 1930s and 1970s, if you supported the popular Demotic you were identified as a decadent and dangerous anti-Greek(!) libertarian; in the later twentieth century, if you used *Katharévousa* you were considered a right-wing nationalist. Result? More riots. This probably sounds like some impossible virtual reality. Welcome to Greece.

A BRIEF HISTORY
Before Homer

So what is the origin of the Greek people? There are no conclusive theories as to when they first emerged as a cultural entity. One certainty is that since their language is probably the oldest continuously spoken tongue in the world, we can use it as a marker for ancientness.

The period c. 2100–1900 BCE is called the Early and Middle Helladic, though (unrelated) farming communities existed around 6000 BCE. In 2000 BCE the Cretans developed multimasted sailing ships; the remnants of their Minoan civilization, with its animated frescos, are still visible. The earliest readable evidence of Greek dates from the Mycenaean empire that produced the Linear B script in around 1500 BCE. Its spoken version goes even further back. Cycladic culture also began thriving in the Aegean. The large fortified palaces in Tyrins and Mycenae were later thought to have been built by giants, the Cyclops; hence the word Cyclopean. The fall of the city of Troy in c. 1193 BCE indicates that the various Greek kingdoms and city-states were a busy lot who could organize large-scale concerted expeditions, in this case under King Agamemnon of the Mycenaeans.

After Homer

For many Greeks and non-Greeks, civilization as we know it begins with the epic poet Homer, whose bearded wisdom set the fashion right up to today's Orthodox priest in your local *ekklesía* (church). According to the historian Herodotus (c. 485–425 BCE), Homer wrote the *Iliad* and the *Odyssey* in c. 850 BCE, though today it is dated earlier at c. 900. They are transcriptions of an earlier oral tradition. These works mark the beginning of literature as we know it, as well as depicting with spine-chilling relevance to the modern reader the human condition in times of turmoil. Their ethical, religious, and historical awareness schooled the Greeks across the ages and continues to this very day. The writings also refer to "barbarophone" people (speaking barbaric languages). Incidentally, the pejorative connotations of the term "barbarian," in antithesis to Hellenes, emerged much later with the works of Thucydides and Plato. In 776 lyric poetry was invented on the island of Paros and the first Olympic Games took place at Olympia, near the western shore of the Peloponnese. From c. 700 Greeks began colonizing the Mediterranean—Marseilles was founded by their colonists c. 600. In around 625 metal coins first appeared showing an ear of wheat and indicating that grains of wheat had once acted as currency. The name of the currency was the *Drachma*, which means "as much as one can hold in the hand," referring to a handful of copper rods (also used as currency).

Classical Greece, 500–400 BCE

The notion of Classical Greece conjures up everything that Western civilization associates as its cultural matrix, from entertainment to sports, politics, the empowerment of the individual, art, literature, rhetoric, architecture, the sciences . . . Greek philosophy set the great themes for the next two millennia. Meanwhile, the archaic statues were losing their formulaic rigidity, animated by the spirit of movement and of mankind at its physical peak. Greek tragedy and theater set the mold for story development as we know it today. All our basic musical terms—rhythm, meter, symphony, chord, choir, guitar, organ, bass— are Greek, including "music," which means "of the muses." There is nothing new today under the Hollywood sun. All this is associated with Athens. Over two thousand years later the poet John Milton wrote in *Paradise Lost*:

> *. . . Where on the Aegean shore a city stands,*
> *Built nobly, pure the air and light the soil,*
> *Athens, the eye of Greece, mother of the arts*
> *And eloquence, native to famous wits . . .*

This was followed in 1821 by Percy Bysshe Shelley's famous statement, "We are all Greeks."

The one historical monument that projects all these achievements in our imagination is found in Athens, at the temple of the Parthenon crowning the Acropolis. Not surprisingly, it was chosen as the symbol for Unesco, and its handling continues to generate intense debate with worldwide implications.

Perhaps the most important political step for humanity was taken by Kleisthenes. He was an Athenian lawmaker and politician (565–500 BCE) who allied himself with the *demos* (the ordinary people), ensuring it was their grassroots concerns that empowered the State. This system was named democracy.

However, wars never stopped. The Persians had begun eyeing the Hellenic lands. In 490 BCE Athens defeated them in the Battle of Marathon. One of the seminal victories in world affairs, it changed the course of history by preventing the Persians from obliterating Hellenic civilization and imposing their Asiatic values on the Greeks. By the time more Persian invasions followed, the

Greeks had learned to arm themselves, and not just with weapons; they used tactics to compensate for their smaller numbers—in other words, muscle backed with brains. After all, Ulysses was revered for his cunning and initiative in the face of insurmountable odds. Also, Olympian gods, like Athena, were revered as defenders of human wisdom. Unhappily, the Greeks themselves excelled at fighting each other with devastating results; at least these bloody wars generated ever greater works of art and literature, sharpening the language and the search for truth according to human values. Thucydides, the author of the account of the Peloponnesian War—in which Athens and Sparta beat each other senseless—insofar as he wrote about contemporary events, could be considered the father of investigative journalism. He researched his subject, spoke to witnesses, and double-checked his sources.

Alexander the Hellenizer

By the time King Philip of Macedonia died in 338 BCE, the northern kingdom of Macedonia had taken advantage of the incessant fighting between its southern neighbors and conquered them. His son, Alexander the Great, decided to move east and build an empire extending as far as the Indus valley. Today, in India, people who have only

vaguely heard of Greece know who Alexander was, together with Aristotle (that is, Aristotle Onassis, not the seminal philosopher who also taught Alexander). He took with him a contingent of teachers and architects and spread Hellenic culture, language, and architecture wherever he went. For a while, Buddhist sculpture was impregnated with Hellenic motifs, including the Buddhas in Afghanistan destroyed by the Taliban. With Alexander's death in 323 BCE the Greeks began fighting each other, and his empire broke up into smaller, Hellenized states. One of those Macedonian families, the Ptolemies, ruled over Egypt as Greek pharaohs until Queen Cleopatra (and her lover, Mark Anthony) committed suicide in 30 BCE, thereby ending the last Hellenic ruling house for many centuries. By then, Greek civilization had spread throughout the Mediterranean and become the predominant culture in the Near East, where the Greek language was the norm. In Alexandria in about 300 BCE Euclid's *Elements*, the basic mathematical textbook for the next 2,000 years, summarized all the mathematical knowledge of the Greeks.

Roman Greece
In effect, the infighting between the Greeks opened the way for the disciplined, though culturally crude, Romans to enter the world stage. In 146 BCE

Corinth was sacked and the Greeks knew who was master of their land. In fact, the Romans were more interested in imposing punishing taxation on their subject people. However, they soon succumbed to Hellenic culture. Their teachers, many of them slaves, were Greek, as were their gods, architecture, and sculpture. Their rather basic and unstructured language adopted Greek grammar and literature, and expanded exponentially with the adoption of Greek words.

Even the Hebrew Bible, the *Torah*, had to be translated into Greek for the, by now Hellenized, Jewish faithful of the Mediterranean Diaspora to understand it—Hebrew having ceased to be a spoken, vernacular tongue. For that matter, King Herod's education was Greek, and Roman officials communicated to the local Judean and Galilean hierarchy in that language.

Constantinople and Byzantium

The collapse of the Roman Empire in the fifth century CE, following the Goth invasions, is considered a landmark in world history, a reminder that nothing lasts forever. But it is a misleading reminder, partly reflecting the regionalism of subsequent Western historians, since the Empire actually lasted for another thousand years. It had split into two, between Roman West and Greek East, after Constantine the Great built his eastern New Rome on the shores of the Bosphorus, where the ancient Greek colony of Byzantium stood. In 330 CE it was dedicated as the new capital of the Roman Empire. His successors named it Constantinople. As the Western empire moved into a period known as the Dark Ages, its Eastern sister thrived. The term Byzantium as synonymous with the Eastern Roman Empire was first used by fifteenth-century Athenian historian Laonikos Chalkokondyles: "the kings of Byzantium were proud to call themselves kings [emperors] of the Romans and did not claim the title king of the Hellenes." (A handful of Chalkokondyles's descendants, after many cosmopolitan adventures, live in Athens today.)

The enfeebling term "Byzantium" was popularized by Western European historians in the nineteenth century, replacing more appropriate appellations such as "Greek Eastern Roman Empire." Here, "Greek" referred both to the actual people and to the language, and especially to the Hellenic roots of the Empire that came to encompass a mosaic of (Latin) Romans, Slavs, Armenians (some of whom became emperors themselves), as well as Arabic-speakers.

Their religion was mostly Eastern Orthodox Christian, as opposed to Roman Catholic Christian in the west. Where the Hellenizing process could not take hold, the educational process took place in the local languages, even if they had to be totally rearranged. So, in the ninth century, the brothers Cyril and Methodius, Greek monks from Thessaloniki, translated the Bible from its original Greek into the Slavonic dialect of the peasants beyond the city's walls. Hence, they began the conversion of the Slavs. In order to accommodate the different sounds of Slavonic, they also invented a special alphabet, Cyrillic (based on the Greek), adapted to the Slavonic pronunciation. This huge cultural, spiritual, and political project had an enduring impact on the Slavic people by harnessing their rudimentary and hugely varying language within the laws of Greek grammar. It also enriched it with the transliteration of Greek words

that did not exist in Slavonic. In effect, this provided a new language in Europe and, with Christianization, it gave birth to nations such as the Bulgarians, Russians, Ukrainians, and others. The great Western "thank you" in 1204 was to divert a Crusade intended to liberate the Holy Lands from the Muslims, which sacked

Constantinople. Though the Empire recovered, it was never the same again—something its enemies knew very well. A lasting divide had opened up between the Orthodox East under the Patriarchate of Constantinople and the Roman Catholic West.

Exiles and the Renaissance

So what did the so-called Byzantines do for us, apart from providing the dynamics that brought into existence a distinct Slavic civilization? For a start, they stabilized the dogma of the Christian religion through a series of Councils. They preserved the classical tradition and through their scholars they communicated it to the Italians from the thirteenth century onward. The flow to Italy of these scholars swelled as exiles and refugees fled the Turkish advances from Asia into Europe. Small colonies were developing in Venice, Florence, Padua, and Bologna. The flow increased as Constantinople neared its fall, in 1453. Together with their advanced teaching skills, their manuscripts and manuals, they fostered the Renaissance. Chalkokondyles educated the Englishmen Linacre and Grocyn, on their visit to fifteenth-century Italy, in the Greek language and the necessary analytical skills to study the Ancients. They, in turn, reimported those skills to Oxford and began a new scholastic tradition in England. On a military level, the Byzantines fought an increasingly losing battle from the sixth century against the Islamic invasions, trying to keep them in check. This allowed Western Europe, still in its infancy, to find its voice and emerge in its own right, relatively secure in its territories north of the Alps. It is wise to avoid presenting the Byzantine achievement as the missing wonder link in world civilization, but the lack of recognition of its role does leave a gaping hole in our understanding of Western and Islamic civilizations. Being in Greece offers a perfect opportunity to explore this legacy.

Though it is not in the scope of this work, Venice also played a pivotal role in Greek affairs, holding on to the Ionian islands as part of its empire, such as Corfu, and clashing with the Turks in the Aegean to control maritime routes. Venice hosted thousands of Greeks—merchants, scholars, and theologians, from the fourteenth to the late eighteenth century—to whom it owes its Byzantine style and an invaluable collection of manuscripts.

Nightmares and Betrayal

Few other countries have had such an intense relationship with betrayal. Greek history contains marked occurrences of callous acts of inter-Greek betrayal and treachery, especially against leading figures and at key historical moments, right up to the Second World War and 1974. For instance, the word for "nightmare" is *efiáltis*; this, however, was the actual name of the person who betrayed the Spartans to the Persians during the Battle of Thermopylae in 480 BCE, thereby losing them the battle and endangering the entire land. There is no other word for nightmare, just the name of a traitor. By far the greatest nightmare in Greek history was the four-hundred-year period of Ottoman rule.

The Ottoman Centuries: Years of Ambiguity
Constantinople fell to the Turks on Tuesday, May 29, 1453. The last Byzantine emperor, Constantine XI Paleologos, died in full armor, defending the sacred wall of the Queen of Cities. Subsequently, the Patriarch was hanged by the invader. The name Istanbul is a phonetic adaptation of the Greek "*eis tin Poli*," which means "to town"—for the Byzantines there was only one city, one *polis*, and that was Constantinople. Even today, Greeks heading for Istanbul, whether on pilgrimage to the Patriarchate, to see their lost parental home, or simply to shop, say, "*páo istin Póli*," "I am going to the City."

The long night of occupation by the Turkish Ottoman empire plunged Greece into a state of slavery for four hundred years, cutting it off from most major developments. The Turks had an alien language, religion, and culture. Yet, to say this fails to do justice to the initial soundness of Ottoman rule. During its rise it had been partially schooled in administrative matters by the Byzantines themselves. The Greek Orthodox Church was also granted, through the Patriarchate of Constantinople, aegis over the Ottoman Christian populations. Hence, the Greek language continued to prevail.

Until the late seventeenth century, Ottoman rule was, in some respects, more tolerant of other religions than the West, where the wars of religion had decimated entire regions. One can speculate that had Vienna fallen to the Ottomans in 1683, much of central Europe would have become Ottoman territory, placed under the administration of Greek governors. Such was the case later on with Moldavia and Wallachia (today's Romania), which was governed on behalf of the Sultans by noble Greek families from 1716 to 1821. Furthermore, the Ottoman navy was largely built by Greek shipwrights, and captained by them. So much so that today's Turkish navy is replete with Greek nautical terms, as well as Venetian and Genoese (also mostly introduced by Greeks trained on their ships). In the nineteenth

century some of the brightest Ottoman
ambassadors and ministers were Greeks.

The dark side of the occupation was that any
sense of initiative was crushed and the concept
erased from memory. People were not in control
of their own destinies. The impact of those
centuries is apparently still palpable in today's
Greece in attitudes toward authority, with many
people feeling that there is one law for them and
no laws for the state and those who run it. Many
Greeks, to this day, still keep shy of the state,
minding their own business.

The Turks also forbade the construction of civil
and ecclesiastic buildings of any substance.
Everything had to be weak enough to be
destroyed by a band of soldiers. Churches were
built at near ground level and their doors were
low so as to prevent cavalry detachments from
desecrating them with their horses. On the other
hand, the greatest architect in the Empire was
Sinan, a Greek Orthodox boy carried away to
Constantinople and made to adopt the Muslim
faith. When he died in 1588 his list of buildings
included the Sulemaniye Mosque, dominating
Istanbul's skyline. His inspiration from Byzantine
churches is obvious and the style spread across
the Ottoman lands.

Non-Muslims were considered *raya* (cattle)
and slaves to the Sultan. He could dispose of them

as he pleased. Hundreds of thousands of lives were lost to such "pleasures," especially as the ethics of the Sultanate began degenerating from the late seventeenth century. There were sporadic massacres and occasional genocides, while pogroms continued beyond 1955, attracting scant concern from the civilized world.

The Forgotten Roads to National Regeneration
At this point, in order to understand something about Greek individuality outside the "antiquity trap" and the four hundred years of oppression, it is worth highlighting some opposite trends. Since the Greek impact on Italy and Eastern Europe is better documented, though little circulated, we will concentrate on Western Europe.

As the wars of religion cut deep wounds across the European continent right up to the end of the seventeenth century, the Orthodox Church proved an important factor. Both the Protestants and the Catholics wished to present their faith as being truly grounded in Christianity's early beginnings. Therefore, whoever could win the Greeks to their side would, in effect, have won a defining moral victory. Matters were all the more alluring since the Greek faith did not have armies of soldiers attached to it, just millions of believers. Greek theologians were sweeping across the Continent, interpreting the Greek texts of the

Bible and the Gospels, teaching their language to scholars, explaining the mysteries. In this respect two Greek Orthodox religious best-sellers impacted on Europe. The first was *Christian Catechism,* by Zacharie Gerganos, in 1622; it attacked the Latin Church and the Pope, and sided with the Protestants. The second was *Refutations,* by Caryophillos, in 1631, defending the Roman Catholic faith.

The Athenian politician and medical doctor Leonardos Philaras (1595–1673) was an advisor to the French court, enjoying the patronage of Cardinal Richelieu. He was also friends with the poet John Milton while the latter held a government post equivalent to Foreign Minister under Cromwell's Commonwealth. He called on him to "excite his armies and his ships to liberate Greece from the Ottoman tyrant." Milton could not possibly engage in such an expedition, so he replied that first the Greeks should prove themselves worthy of such a mission. On the other hand, he eagerly sought Philaras's medical advice on his deteriorating eyesight.

Finally, most of us sport a rounded scar on our arm or thigh from our childhood vaccination against smallpox. This method of immunization was developed and placed on a scientific basis by two Constantinople-based physicians, Emmanuel Timonis and Iacovos Pylarinos, who produced scientific papers on the subject, published in the West by the Royal Society in London in 1712 and 1715. The practice was widely used among the poorer and peasant classes in the area of Andrianoupolis (Edirne) and in Thessaly— invariably by Greek Orthodox women associated with a local church, which offered blessings and profited from the sale of special candles. The earliest reference to vaccination goes back to the island of Cephalonia in the sixteenth century. The first written description of acquired immunity comes from Thucydides, where he explains that those who survived the Plague of Athens in 430 BCE did not catch it again.

The list of similarly forgotten personalities can fill several volumes. Their absence from the European Valhalla of personages worth remembering is puzzling. Perhaps European pride feels that memorable Hellenes are best plucked from antiquity, without bringing on to the scene those active during the last two millennia.

... and 1821

The Greek war of independence was declared on March 25, 1821 at Kalavrita in the Peloponnese. This national revolution marks the entry of Greece into the modern European family. Memories of the event still engage and inspire local amateur historians.

LIVING HISTORY

Consider, at a microcosmic level, the impact of that event. Dr. Panos Papadopoulos's (1900–92) ancestor fought in the 1821 insurrection. His family is from neighboring Akrata village, tucked beneath Mt. Helmos where the mythical river Styx runs and where the infant Achilles was plunged into its immortal waters. Akrata was also the scene of one of the first independence battles. Dr. Panos's modest family archives and his own published research reveal that the Revolution broke out on March 14, but that the date was subsequently moved forward for the uprising to include as participants certain political families that turned up after the event. As for the Doctor, he was a pioneer of Greek oncology, who in the Second World War acted as a doctor in the resistance against the occupying Axis forces.

The passion for justice and human rights runs deep in the family; his daughter, Eleni Pambouki, was a pioneer of women's rights in Greece after the fall of the junta, and opened the country's first women's bookshop. Her daughter, Maria, became the high priestess responsible for igniting the Olympic Flame at Olympia (down the road from Kalavrita). And yet, this is an ordinary Greek family.

There are many similar, amateur historians in Greece who will go to great lengths to publish and distribute privately their meticulous research. If you find one with whom you can communicate, it is worth whiling away an evening with them for a unique and highly personalized snapshot of regional history.

The fact is that not only did the uprising take place, it transformed the course of the Ottoman Empire. Many European *philhéllenes* (friends of the Greeks, their world, and their cause), such as Lord Byron, journeyed there to join their fight for liberation. It may surprise the reader to learn that though the Greeks were the first to set the pattern for the dissolution of the Ottoman Empire, the last country to emerge out of its remains was the Turkish Republic itself, in 1922.

The Triumph, Chimera, and Pain of Independence

Greece was finally recognized as a nation-state in 1829. In some respects, its fate lay in the hands of the Great Powers; these were Britain (whose start-up loan to the country had it paying interest until the twentieth century), fellow Orthodox

Russia, and, to a lesser extent, France. They also imposed an absolutist monarchical system on the country with a Bavarian prince, Otto, as its first King. The people would have preferred the American model. He was removed in 1862 only to be replaced by a German-Danish dynasty whose members were repeatedly forced into exile and returned through dubious referenda. Economically, Greece was 65 percent agricultural, and failed to improve productivity until the First World War.

Since the late eighteenth century the dream of uniting all the historically Hellenic lands was alive. The political activist and author Rhigas Ferraios, from Thessaly, campaigned for a Balkan republic, united by the Greek language (it was the language of business and the intelligentsia) and where all ethnic groups, of all religions, could live freely and in mutual respect. He was arrested by the Austrians in 1797 and handed over to the Turkish authorities, who executed him without trial. After independence this dream, rebranded as the "*Megáli Idéa*" ("Great Idea-vision"), success-fully guided Greece's foreign policy for a while.

Following their gains during the Balkan Wars in 1912–13 and their support of the Allies in the First World War, the Greeks reacquired in 1921 most of Ionia in Anatolia, including what the Turks called "*Giaour Izmir*" ("infidel Smyrna"), and their forces were only a few miles away from Constantinople. All this, with the encouragement of the victorious powers. Then, nemesis and betrayal set in. The promises of support from the Allies failed to materialize. They had secured the Middle East from the Turks, and the Greeks were left to their fate. The government pressed on against the Turks, overstretching its supply lines, and the tide turned dramatically. The Greek troops were pushed back, cosmopolitan Smyrna was burned down, and while Allied ships stood by in the bay thousands were massacred in the smoldering ruins. Three thousand years of Greek presence was wiped out in days. The refugee song stating "*the earth turned black and wiped out your name*," was based on fact, not poetic interpretation. Among the refugees were Aristotle Onassis and Alexander Issigonis, the future inventor of the Mini car. The memory is seared into the Greek experience as the *Megáli Katastrophí* (Great Catastrophe–a word that literally means "a downward change"). The war marked the end of the Ottoman Empire and the birth of the Turkish Republic. In the ensuing forced exchange of populations more than one million Anatolian Greek Orthodox were sent into Greece, swelling the population by a fifth. One in four children under the age of five died from the hardships. Families were forever scattered. In the Pontus (northeastern Turkey) genocide against the Pontian Greeks saw the extermination of up to 300,000. The Armenians fared much worse with the loss of nearly 1.5 million. The Greek word "holocaust" (wholesale destruction by fire) existed long before becoming the definition of horror during the Second World War. The earlier holocaust of Chios marked the 1822 destruction of this prosperous island. Likewise we have the holocaust of Smyrna in 1922. And for the Greeks, what was done, was done and cannot be erased.

The Second World War
There is one thing to remember about Greece's participation in the Second World War. While the rest of Europe, apart from Britain, was under Axis control or neutral, Greece was ordered to surrender or face destruction. That seemed a logical demand: the country was isolated, its ruler, the dictator Metaxas, admired the Fascist methods (not their racism), and the Axis was unstoppable. Greece went against all expectations. On October 28, 1940, a direct, laconic, uncompromising reply was issued: "*OXI*" (pronounced "ochi" and meaning "no"). Immediately Mussolini invaded. The Greek army, backed by hundreds of women carrying light artillery through the snow and up precipitous passes, pushed the invader back across the Albanian border, gaining territory. This was

the first victory against the Axis. In Britain, the news came as a breath of fresh air.

By the spring of 1941, Hitler decided he had to intervene, thereby crucially delaying his attack against Russia closer to the winter. This time the country was conquered. Soon the first act of European resistance took place in Athens, by the teenagers Glezos (now an MP) and Santos. In the winter of 1942 as many as 300,000 people died of starvation. In total, Greece lost over one-tenth of its population in the 1940s—the highest percentage in Europe. Even as times were desperate and the Germans began rounding them up to send them into forced labor, what did the starving Greeks do? They went on strike against these measures. Up in the mountainous countryside, and like their ancestors had done with the Turks, the *andártes*, or partisans, gained control of vast expanses of territory.

The Civil War

Sadly, by 1943 the first signs of a civil war became apparent. The anti-German resistance coalesced around two movements. By far the larger was EAM–ELLAS, consisting of different political persuasions but led by the Communists. The other was EDES, attracting mostly right-wing elements. With the near certainty of Allied victory, they began clashing with each other. The antagonism was further fueled by the British and later the Americans. At Yalta in February 1945 Churchill, Roosevelt, and Stalin carved up the postwar world into spheres of interest. Greece was earmarked for the Western camp; all left-wing resistance had to be eliminated.

During 1946–49 a bitter civil war raged between the Communist-dominated left and the British- and American-backed government forces. This became the first clash of the Cold War. It also brought the U.S.A. firmly into Greek political life, distorting the dynamics of Greek society. All this polarized the people right up to the 2004 elections. Today, we can say that the result of those elections has buried the ghosts of those years, even though they still lurk in the rhetoric of some politicians, and in the pages of one of the country's most popular "intellectual" newspapers.

1950–74: Light at the End of the Tunnel

The civil war over, the country became a founding member of NATO in 1954. Due to the Cold War conditions, anti-left paranoia was in full swing in the West. The aggressive polarization of left and right in world politics was as merciless as it was unsophisticated. In Greece there were arrests of so-called subversive elements, internal exile, and constant interventions in its internal affairs by the U.S.A. Right-wing governments succeeded each other. The army was royalist and escaped political control. In 1964, a victory at the polls by the Union of the Center (politically ranging from left of center to truly left) was quickly overturned, both by splits in its own ranks and especially by the King and his supporters. This triggered a period of political chaos.

Paradoxically, the economy began flourishing, boosted by the Greek merchant marine. The hundreds of thousands of Greeks forced by economic circumstances to emigrate also sent back remittances to their families, swelling the coffers of the state.

In 1967 a coup took place by the military and Greece was ruled by a junta. In 1974, with the apparent blessing of Washington, it backed a right-wing coup in the Republic of Cyprus initiated by local Greek-Cypriots against President Archbishop Makarios. Turkey intervened, also with Washington's blessing, on the grounds of protecting the Turkish Cypriot minority, and occupied nearly half the island. The Athens junta collapsed within days and Greece finally gained a truly democratic regime. The short-lived monarchy was abolished by referendum—enough was enough, irrespective of political allegiance. In the 1990s, President Clinton apologized to the

Greek people for America's obstructive role in their affairs.

A European Pioneer

In 1981, Greece became the tenth member of the European Community (now the EU), transforming itself into a relatively wealthy state. In fact, it did not meet the economic criteria; much catching up was needed. But political mastermind Constantinos Karamanlis made full use of his European political connections; Athens argued that membership to the European Community would guarantee the survival of its newly regained democracy. It worked. These arguments would later be applied for the accession of Spain, Portugal, and the former Eastern European countries; the latter wished to join the EU for reasons of stability and security from their former Soviet masters.

The Greek political scene, though, from 1981 to 2004, was dominated by the socialist PASOK Party, until its electoral defeat in 2004. Even so, it continues to dominate many aspects of institutional and media life because most of the key positions were filled with its supporters. Its longevity reflected the electorate's exasperation with right-wing governments, and, unfortunately, the populist rhetoric of some of its leaders exploited the polarization of Greek society for political gain. It also gained a reputation of fostering unprecedented levels of corruption across society, especially in its dealings with government institutions and the allotment of contracts. Most official positions, be they in the civil service or state-owned enterprises, were filled (or rather, shockingly overstaffed) according to political affiliation and personal contacts. You could say that each position was filled by three people, unqualified and unwilling to carry it out—many of whom also held other jobs. The tenure of Civil Servants is constitutionally guaranteed and outrageously costly to the taxpayer.

Finally, it is worth remembering that Greece was the smallest country to take on responsibility for the largest global event, the Olympic Games. They took place in Athens in 2004, at the most challenging of times. The practicalities had not been thought through to the end, and after the 9/11 attacks the security challenge was overwhelming, but with such a heritage some obligations cannot be counted. You assume them or you don't. Greeks around the word said "yes"; Greeks in Greece are still paying the bill.

GOVERNMENT AND POLITICS
Overview

Greece is a Parliamentary Democracy, *Koinobouleftiki Demokratia.* Though one can also say that it is a Parliamentary Republic, because the term *demokratia* translates as both democracy and republic. It is headed by a president elected by parliament. The prime minister and the government hold executive powers. The Constitution of Greece is the official Charter of the State. It was voted and ratified in 1975. The parliament consists of 300 deputies—far too many for the size of its population (proportionately, a country like the U.K. would have 1,800 MPs instead of its current 659). Most of them simultaneously hold down other jobs. Voting is a right and a constitutional obligation.

Anyone can run for the presidency if he or she has been a Greek citizen for at least five years. The role of President of the Republic is mostly symbolic and transcends party politics. The president is empowered to represent the state internationally. He, or she, cannot dissolve or convene Parliament, declare war, or issue decrees.

Greek officials have a low sense of responsibility; this is ultimately referred forever up the ranks to the ministers and the prime minister—who can then, often legitimately, wash their hands of anything distasteful.

The Art of Influencing

How can you influence someone at a deep level without bribing them? After the Olympic bribery scandals involving candidate cities and the International Olympic Committee were revealed in the 1990s, the Greek Olympic bidding team faced a strategic challenge. Under the leadership of Gianna Angelopoulou, a solution was found. She invited members of the IOC (known as the "immortals") to the relaxing grandeur of her homes in Athens and London. There, she told them, "Please allow me to give you a present. I know that presents are not allowed, but I hope that you and the Olympic Committee will forgive me; could you wait a second while I fetch it?" She then left and returned with a handsome envelope for each IOC guest. Inside was a copy of the *New York Times*, issued on their date of birth. This, inevitably, moved them; they took the newspapers to an adjacent room and spend some time reading about the events that occurred on the day they were born. It was something unique in their lives, unforgettable, and certainly not a bribe.

Challenges or Problems?

You see it but will probably fail to notice it, because we still hold the notion that countries like Italy and Greece love children. In fact, both countries have one of the lowest birthrates in the world, briefly moving into negative growth. The Greek electorate is ageing: the average age is forty-four; soon it will reach fifty-four. The pension burden means there is growing risk of poverty for the over-sixty-fives. Extremely urgent reforms are postponed. In 2001 a proposal was put forward to avert a "fiscal apocalypse," but withdrawn.

This is where the EU comes in handy. Wiser politicians of both main parties use the country's EU membership and duties to bypass local opposition and propose the unthinkable in terms of fiscal reforms. However, one reform was the introduction of cheap mortgages in a country that had hardly experienced this phenomenon and where personal debts were at a record low. Today, too many Greeks seem newly and heavily indebted, though still blissfully unaware of the implications.

Forward in a Complex Neighborhood
Greece is seen as an ideal location and as a base for Western companies to explore and expand into the wider region. They also recruit Greek businessmen and entrepreneurs whose regional skills are eminently adapted to the different negotiating cultures, from Romania to Turkey and the Middle East, and to the art of undertaking transactions.

In the 1990s, during the early stages of the crisis in the former Yugoslavia, Athens imposed an ill-thought embargo against "Yugoslav Macedonia." But Greek businessmen found ways to break it to sustain their markets. Gradually, with each succeeding Balkan crisis in Bosnia, Albania, and Kosovo, Athens realized it needed to strengthen its regional ties. It even helped in the creation of a multinational Balkans force to participate in regional peace support operations. In September 1999 the Multinational Peace Force Southeastern Europe (MPFSEE) was activated in Plovdiv, Bulgaria. The brigade, which comprises Albania, Bulgaria, Greece, Italy, the former Yugoslav Republic of Macedonia, Romania, and Turkey, aims either to operate under the auspices of NATO or the UN, or to act independently.

In January 2004 the first Balkan forum of bank unions for all Balkan countries was held in Athens. The aim of the forum was to exchange information and start constructive dialogue on issues concerning the banking system in the broader region of southeast Europe.

Greece is also a neighbor of the volatile Middle East. Here it has developed a sensitive and constructive approach, balancing the rights of the Palestinians and Israel's security concerns, its duties toward its Western allies with its own regional needs, duties, and experiences.

Relations with the Balkans

Greece is first and foremost interested in promoting unequivocal regional stability. Compared to its neighbors, within its broader neighborhood, it stands out as a beacon of democratic values and sound economic principles. Today, echoing its pioneering role across the centuries in setting a leading example in the political, cultural, and economic fields, Greek entrepreneurs have become the most important investors in the region. Athens is the most ardent supporter of its neighbors joining the EU—including giving support for Turkish membership. This constant interaction is invaluable to the region. It exposes it to Western standards of negotiating and doing business, with the added bonus that Greece's intermediate technology skills are eminently suited to "beginners" in the market economy.

One thing you will hear about concerns the huge influx of immigrants from Albania. They arrived after 1991, when this once isolated (and unmissed) bastion of authoritarian Communism collapsed. Admittedly, up to 20 percent of the newcomers belonged to the persecuted Greek minority concentrated in southern Albania (geographically known as northern Epirus).

Most of the Albanians completely lacked any sense of civic responsibility and were unskilled, beyond the basic requirements of their long outdated infrastructure. Up to 800,000 have entered Greece, illegally. Problems were inevitable and they have introduced unprecedented levels of crime. A recent CIA report describes Albania as having high unemployment, a dilapidated infrastructure, and widespread gangsterism. However, they provided the country with cheap labor. In return, many of them are gradually being granted green cards; they are learning useful trades, their children receive free schooling, and they are being eased into the ways of the modern world. The equivalent for Britain would involve receiving and accommodating six million immigrants in the space of ten years: unthinkable and impossible. But the Greek lands have long experienced massive influxes of populations in search of safety or a better standard of living. The Greeks themselves until recently took to the four corners of the world for a better life. It is an accepting country where the far right scores so low in the polls (less than 1 percent) that it hardly registers.

As for the problem with the former Yugoslav Republic of Macedonia, the debate is over the name. Athens wants its northern neighbor to add something after its name in order to distinguish it from its own, historical province of Macedonia. History explains quite well the reasons for such a seemingly incongruous concern. Otherwise, the two countries get along well, with Greece offering full humanitarian support to the Slav Macedonians when they had to face attacks from local and Kosovar Albanians in 1999.

Turkey: Between Crisis and Opportunities
Most people think they know it. Greeks and Turks: cats and dogs. They have always hated each other, right? Not exactly. Today's Greeks simply fear being invaded by the Turks; too many people are still alive and remember the persecutions. In 1953, Turkey made life impossible for the Greek inhabitants of the islands of Imbros and Tenedos. In September 1955, anti-Greek pogroms in Istanbul succeeded in reducing the native Greek Orthodox population from over 100,000 to less than 3,000. Most fled, taking with them nothing but the clothes they were wearing. The scale of persecution was reminiscent of the anti-Jewish assaults during Kristallnacht in Germany in 1938, but it remained ignored by the international community. Businesses, houses, assets, and properties worth billions of dollars (in today's money) were lost and have yet to be returned. People were murdered, even more raped and beaten. It is impossible to ignore the impact of such barbaric behavior. Then, in the 1980s, Ankara began claiming a host of Greek islands

and half the Aegean. To top it off, Turkey constantly denies that the Armenian genocide took place, stating that it was a well-deserved response to their uprising. Only supporters of genocide as a political tool could laugh at Greek concerns.

No animosity extends to the ordinary people of Turkey, who are often viewed as victims of Ankara's military-dominated regime. During the disastrous earthquakes that struck both countries in 1999, the rush to help one another was swift, generous, and, especially, spontaneous. Overall, the fear of Turkish intentions is almost an appropriate reaction. However, the Athenian state and media seem to cultivate an unhealthy ignorance of this powerful, complex, and militaristic neighbor. Recently, though, there has been a calculated rapprochement, including Greece's full support for Turkish EU membership. Today, Greek tourism in Turkey is the second or third largest, both in numbers and in spending.

The Republic of Cyprus and the "TRNC"
Cyprus is an emotive and costly issue for Greece. The island was under Ottoman dominion for three hundred years, and from 1875 to 1960 under British rule. In normal circumstances London should have respected its commitment to hand the island to Greece as a "reward" for its participation

in the First World War. Instead it chose to "divide and rule" in the 1950s, when many Greek Cypriots fought for *Enosis* (union) with Greece. It never happened. Today, we have two independent nation-states, which are intent on remaining so. In 1974 a Greek-Cypriot coup took place on the island with the blessing of the short-lived Athens junta. It was not against the Turkish Cypriots, but, in true internecine style, it aimed to overthrow the Cypriot democratic government. Ankara responded with the "Attila" invasion in three waves, even as it was negotiating at the UN. It occupies 37 percent of the island to this day, which it calls the Turkish Republic of Northern Cyprus, or TRNC. Over 200,000 Greek Cypriots became refugees, 1,600 are considered as "disappeared," and 100,000 Turkish settlers have turned the local Turkish Cypriots into a new minority. However, the Turkish Cypriots state they feel safer as a separate entity than they would in a union dominated by their southern neighbors.

Since the 1990s, Athens has devoted much of its international negotiating time to promoting the Cyprus issue; the Greek Cypriots have taken full advantage of this and, it could be observed, offered little in return. The policy was based on a simple formula: "Cyprus decides and Greece acquiesces." Athens negotiated hard within the EU institutions and among fellow EU members for

Cypriot membership. It did this often to the detriment of its own more pressing economic difficulties, or to the rights of thousands of its own refugees. Its concern was based on a feeling of vulnerability of the Hellenic community in the region. But in April 2004, after decades of futile international negotiations, both Cypriot sides agreed to hold a referendum on the latest UN plan, which enjoyed the backing of the EU, Greece, Turkey, and the U.S.A. After years of being the spoilers of negotiations, the Turkish Cypriots accepted the plan and the world praised them. The Greek Cypriots rejected it, thereby suddenly finding themselves burdened with the opprobrium of not wanting a solution. The aging Cypriot government refused to take responsibility for a huge diplomatic defeat, largely of its own making. Instead it blamed the world for having "stitched it up" with a plan that offered no convincing security guarantees.

In May 2004, the Republic of Cyprus became a full member of the EU, with only the wealthy, southern, Greek Cypriot side enjoying the benefits. The island remains divided; 35,000 Turkish troops still occupy the north, only now many sadly consider that their presence has been sanctioned by the Greek Cypriot "no" to the referendum.

chapter two

VALUES &
ATTITUDES

ROMIOSÝNI INTERTWINED WITH HELLENISM

For a meaningful insight into the Greek psyche and its substrate, take a look at *Romiosýni* (pronounced, ro-mee-o-*seen*i). Even better, ask different friends or even acquaintances what the word means to them. Here we are entering a sort of archaeology of the emotions, a world of feeling and attitudes ill-served by brief definitions. You need songs, poetry, stories, lifestyle, and much more to glimpse its references.

Anyhow, here is one view. It originates from the word "Rome" and first emerged after the collapse of the Roman Empire in the West in the fifth century and the continuation of the Eastern Roman Empire (Byzantium). The term seemed to gain wider currency in the sixteenth century and was used by the Greeks themselves and the Ottoman Turks to refer to the Greek Orthodox, Greek-speaking inhabitants of the Ottoman Empire. The Turks adopted it as *Rum* and to this day they use it to indicate the Greek people. Since the 1821 War of Independence some Greeks have associated *Romiosýni* with poverty, subjection (to the Romans and Turks), to popular songs and rebellion; it has also been used to indicate the modern, spoken, popular Greek language, as opposed to its classical version. *Romiosýni* is the real Greek soul as it survived on its wits through the harshest of times. It has inspired some of the finest songs and poems in the culture. For many, it seems to draw the line between the cold, rational West and the more real East.

For the last twenty years, however, the word has retreated, partly because Greeks have become true, if uncomfortable, citizens of Europe—even though *Romiosýni* has also been used to highlight the nation's westernizing tendency. Few words are so laden with meaning.

FAMILY FIRST

Family comes first. In Homer, the prime moral obligation of an individual is to his kin. Today, to the Greeks, family still means the extended family. You may be a nobody to the world; in your family you are somebody. You are gossip to the aunts, the beginning and the end to the grandparents. In the English language "family" means the nuclear family—father, mother, and children. The children grow up, leave, and all that remains of the links are often polite visits. A good example to highlight the distance between the two cultures is the Greek man who ended his engagement with his English fiancée because she could not understand that his uncle's death was important, and that he had to go to the funeral and stay for the forty days' *mnymósino* (remembrance).

Statistics tell us that 72 percent of Greeks actually desire to live in the same house as their children and their parents, with an uncle or aunt thrown in. Often you will come across buildings where all the apartments are occupied by members of the same family. One of the reasons is that most parents will do their utmost to buy a house for all their offspring, and it will be next door. In this respect, the ending to the film *My Big Fat Greek Wedding* was spot on.

The following may surprise you. A number of students studying abroad (mostly in Britain)

occasionally receive fully cooked food parcels by courier from Mother. When the exam season approaches, Mother moves in, cooks, takes care of all their needs, and stands as bodyguard against any distractions. In the process she takes a good survey of the people her offspring has been associating with. Family ties are one of the main reasons that the nanny state did not develop in Greece.

Families have rows, and make life impossible for each other, especially if living in the same house. Children, even when middle-aged, cannot assert themselves with their parents, and parents do not keep to their boundaries. Boundaries? What boundaries? Surely they are a sign that you do not love your children. Everyone longs for open spaces but returns to the fold, for what is there outside it? Call it dysfunctional, if you like—here, more often than not, the dysfunctional functions. Until recently in Greece there were hardly any psychologists. Instead there were too many lawyers.

The best advice is never to speak overcritically about a person to someone else: it could be his or her second cousin, which is important because it means that their parents are first cousins and their grandparents brother and sister. Admittedly, and sadly, these bonds are slackening in the Athenian jungle, though the situation is still a far cry from the collapse of the extended family in the West.

GREEK MOTHERS

Traditionally, thousands of Greeks study abroad. They enable the country to synchronize its ways with those of the wider world. This has sharpened the observation powers of Greek mothers. One student, the story goes, was sharing a house with a female friend. His mother came to visit him and he assured her that there was nothing going on between him and the lady. The mother took the point. When she left, the friend complained that her silver tray had disappeared. So the student wrote to his mother, "Dear Mama, I am not saying that you took the silver tray; I am not saying that you didn't, but an hour before you left it was on the mantelpiece." The mother replied, "My dear child, I am not saying that you are sleeping with that girl, I am not saying that you are not, but if she was sleeping in her own bed, she would have found it under her blanket."

Another story concerns the student who becomes engaged. His mother flies over to meet the future bride, so the son holds a small garden party. As he is about to find his fiancée to introduce her, mother tells him not to worry, she will locate her. Five minutes later she returns and points out a particular girl. "How did you know?" exclaims the son. Mother shakes her head, "I didn't like her," she says.

HIERARCHY

There are hardly any class divisions in Greece. Many story lines in films shot between the 1950s and the 1970s tell of poor boy/girl falling for rich girl/boy. Love conquers all and the parents are happy, everyone has a future together. As a rule, the father heads the family, while the *yiayiá* (grandmother) and mother often rule the roost. At work hierarchies can be blurred, especially if it is a family-run business (be it a small shop or a multimillion-dollar shipping enterprise). Ultimate responsibility rests with the boss, and this could be the uncle or some other relative, so if he has introduced a junior in your office, that junior is accountable to him and there is nothing you can do about it. In that respect, you, in a way, come second to him or her.

One area Greeks pay attention to concerns the chairpersons of even the smallest organizations. They are addressed as *Kýrie* or *Kyría Próedre* (Mr. or Mrs. President) even outside their functions. Ex-ministers never lose their title. Doctors are addressed as *Iatreý*, and teachers or lecturers (especially male) as *Kýrie Kathigité*.

PERSONAL RELATIONSHIPS

If you want to develop your personal support system, then get into personal relationships. Keep in regular touch with those you like, not forgetting those you need. This is not networking American-style. It can provide you with daily support, such as in your expeditions to sort something out with the Kafkaesque bureaucracy; it can find shortcuts for those small jobs that seem to take ages in Greece. Personal relationships are the manna, the lubricant of everyday life. Among Greeks they can also occasion outbursts of seemingly destructive fury.

GENEROSITY

The Greek word is *geneodoría*, literally "brave at giving presents." There is no discernible pattern in what triggers the famed Greek generosity—which goes hand in hand with hospitality. It happens haphazardly, on the spur of the moment. You go out shopping for a couple of oranges and the seller will let you have them for nothing. You are sitting at the local *kafeneíon,* and your landlord spots you on his way to the market and pays your bill. If you show up at someone's house and they are about to eat, they will more than likely invite you in and share the meal. An extra plate is laid, food lands on it, a glass is filled for you, and "*kalós órises*" ("welcome"). No one is after anything from you. The best response is to go with the flow and spread some of it around yourself.

GREEK PROVERBS

"Live together or be hanged separately."

"The head that bows cannot be chopped off."

"When you hear there are cherries a-plenty, take a small basket." (In other words, disbelieve big promises.)

"Better five in hand than ten in the bush."

"A favor done quickly is twice done."

"In the land of the blind, the one-eyed is king."

"A present from an enemy is no different from damage."

"It's all salt and beans." (To those who pretend to know with certainty what they can merely guess; it comes from the ceremony of the ancient diviners, who threw salt and beans before predicting the future.)

"Better to have a wise enemy than a crazy friend."

"A madman threw a stone in the well and a hundred wise men could not get it out."

"They are like two donkeys quarreling in a foreign barn."

"He is trying to get the snake out of its hole with the madman's hand."

ATTITUDES TO FOREIGNERS

The word *xénos* in Greek means both foreigner and guest. Tellingly, the West only adopted the word "xenophobe," or fear (*phobia*) of the stranger or foreigner. But there is also *philoxenía*, whose translation into "hospitality" does not do it justice. Maybe you can guess its full meaning: "friend of the stranger/foreigner." There is also *xenomanía*, the exaggerated attraction to all things foreign, usually Western. So it may be that the wealthy family that invites you to their exotic house is not expressing a wholehearted appreciation of your personality. Rather, you, as a Nordic specimen, are there to boost your hosts' status (and their harmless obsession). A famous 1936 satirical song by Kofiniotis, titled "Xenomania," concerned the then current fashion for adopting some English words and for changing their own Greek accents, "*állaxan oi trópoi, gíname Európi*" ("manners have changed, now we are Europe").

As a rule, people feel closer to their fellow Mediterranean and Latin American visitors—Italians, Spanish, and even the French—rather than to the Germans, English, and Americans. Overall, there is an acceptance that foreigners are different and that allowances should be made for them. Greece is very good at accommodating different types. Some resorts like Benitses and

Faliraki fill up with drunken hordes from northern Europe, mainly Brits. Like pigeons in Trafalgar Square, they are contained, and make a mess of the place. The locals display remarkable forbearance toward this yearly invasion; they believe that in their own country the visitors are emotionally repressed and need to go crazy once a year—a sort of Aristotelian catharsis. Until the 1940s, Westerners were referred to by the generic term of *Frángoi*—it probably originates from the thirteenth-century Crusader invasions and means Franks. In Thailand, the same word is used, *farhang;* it was introduced by Constantine Gerakis (Phaulkon), a seventeenth-century deck boy from Cephalonia who rose to become that country's Prime Minister under King Narai.

You will also hear strong condemnation of Americans; by this they mean U.S. policies and it does not affect personal relations. The British, as opposed to North Americans and Australians, are seen as frugal.

CONSPIRACY THEORIES

Welcome to the land of vibrant debates and conspiracy theories (though, if you want the real Disneyland of conspiracy theories go to Albania or Serbia). You can provide many a Greek with the best analyses of a situation, redolent with juicy

GREEKS ON SUPERPOWERS

To understand twenty-first-century Greek
suspicions of the powerful, you only need
to read the Melian Debate in Thucydides's
The Peloponnesian War. Here, for "Athens"
read the United States or any other power;
for "Melos" read a smaller country invaded
or occupied.

In 430 BCE, Athens was an expanding
empire, at war with Sparta. It sailed its fleet
to occupy the neutral island of Melos. But
the Athenians, proud of their democracy,
gave the islanders the chance to argue their
case. The Melians replied that Athens had
already chosen its course of action, and they
were being presented with a "no-win"
situation. They said, "if *our* arguments prove
we are right, you will wage war against us; if
your arguments are right, we will become
your slaves [in other words, you will exploit
us to the hilt]."

Athens chastised them for being so
suspicious, pointing out that such reasoning
was always used by the weak and that the
standard of justice depended on the balance
of power—in this case Athens was the
superpower. The Melians counterargued that
is was in Athens's self-interest to exhibit fair
play and just dealings, in case it lost the war

and needed to enjoy similar treatment itself. Athens responded that losing was not an option and that it would act for the good of the empire. Furthermore, if the Melians gave in they would avert disaster and the Athenians would be able to profit from them.

The Melians pleaded to remain neutral *and* obliging friends. Athens said, "no," because Melian friendship in this context would signal to other nations that Athens was weak. On the other hand, Athens argued, Melian hatred would show the world that Athens was powerful.

The outcome: Melos was destroyed. Athens eventually lost the war.

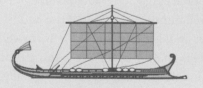

fact; he will ponder, express agreement, move on to a couple of queries, ask a killer of a question, and develop a counter-explanation. Conspiracy theories are usually applied to the powerful, like the U.S. A., their own government, occasionally to the Catholic Church, and to those who have intervened in their affairs, like Britain, France, Europe, and Russia. It is a question of "they are strong, we are weak; they are self-interested, we cannot trust them." Greeks can eloquently speculate on who is behind a policy, and especially, "*pou to páei?*" ("what is he up to?"). Often, such speculation sounds plausible, there is logic and it is seemingly factual; you may well discover that your average blue-collar coffee drinker in Thessaloniki, Larisa, Patras, or Patmos is far better informed about world developments than your average postgraduate student. His/her mercurial mind is quick to put two and two together and come up with various answers.

There is an infuriating side to this attitude; it fosters indolence when it comes to actually doing some deeper research. It is easier to spin accusations through speculative talk. The media thrives on it and some politicians build a government on the back of it. It can happen that if you are good at your job—especially a reporter, a country analyst, an academic—then someone may finger you and accuse you of working for some secret service. Otherwise, how could you possibly know what you do? An American diplomat based in Athens said he would play games trying to guess what the next big conspiracy theory would be.

WEALTH, MONEY, AND THE *VOLEMÉNOS*

An Athenian taxi driver confessed on his way to Piraeus that the type of man he was really jealous of was the *voleménos*. There is no translation for it. It refers to the person who has landed a job he did not earn, the one who, from a nobody and through party or family connections or friends, was given a desk, a chair, and now draws a salary with his pension guaranteed, often at the age of fifty-five. He has a town apartment, a Japanese car, goes on vacation with the family (if married) or with his *paréa* (band of chums). No questions asked, no worries, just minding his business.

As for wealth, the rich are not quite as isolated from the not-so-rich as in many other countries. Besides, Greeks have developed the art of living well with little; perhaps it results from their system of mutual support and the ability to enjoy life's little pleasures in a beautiful climate. The modern Greek literary hero Zorba was just about penniless—but his attitude made him rich. Henry Miller observed that, even clad in rags, a Greek carries them like a king. This is not to say that money is despised. On the contrary, but somehow the Greeks prefer spending it. A London Jewish factory owner told his Greek employee, who was about to start his own business, that the difference between Jews and Greeks is that whereas the Jew earns ten and spends nine, the Greek earns ten and spends eleven.

PATRIOTISM

For a nation that loves a good laugh, you will not hear jokes about the flag or the national anthem. But you will encounter regional pride. This man's village produces the best feta cheese in the world, that one comes from where the best oranges are grown. You may even hear, especially if you are from an English-speaking country, that when you still lived in trees, they were building the Parthenon. Having said that, you will also hear, in the same breath, the fiercest criticism of Greeks from Greeks themselves. Here the general rule of when being abroad applies: keep your comments to yourself, at least until you understand certain parameters of local sensitivities. This being Greece, you are welcome to ask and to query attitudes. After all, you are a foreigner and many Greeks appreciate that you are owed an explanation. In this respect, Greece is an easy and open country.

ARPA-COLA: LAST-MINUTE CULTURE

Three months before the 1994 European Summit in Corfu, there was no road to speak of between the main town and the hotels where thousands of officials and the media were staying. By the time of the summit, the road was ready. In 2000 all the EU countries were ready to join the euro currency zone. Only Greece did not meet the criteria—even with all the numbers cooked. Two years later its finances were in order (or, like the French, convincingly cooked). Greece joined the euro zone with everyone else in 2002. This is Greece, where things materialize just as the curtain is rising. Why? One Greek puts it down to institutionalized inefficiency.

Many jobs are slapdash affairs, or as the Greeks say, *arpa-cola* ("grab 'n paste"). Could this be a legacy from the Ottoman days? For many, there is a sense that nothing you do will be appreciated; that tomorrow is a long way off; as long as by the end of the day it works, and if it does not, well, blame the system. On the other hand, it remains a wonder how, once inside the pressure cooker, things materialize, seemingly out of nothing.

Dancing to Deadlines

Only six months before the Olympic Games and severely behind schedule, the Mayor of Athens,

Dora Bacogianni, was asked why she believed that
her city would be ready on time. She replied, "In
Greece, we are like the '*Sirtaki*' dance; we start
very slowly, and then we speed up. And then at the
end, you cannot even follow how quickly it goes.
So I believe that's exactly what happened with
us . . . We might be afraid until the last minute,
but I believe that we will be ready in time." They
were, and the world marveled.

WOMEN

On the one hand, Greek society is family-based
and women tend to rule the roost; they also
own around 40 percent of the country's private
assets. On the other hand, women, compared to
other European nations, North America,
and Australia are noticeably
underrepresented in politics and
in socioeconomic decision
making. Furthermore, women
were active in the national
and liberation struggles, but
when the fight was over, it was back to the coop.
The question is, if Greek women take similar
career paths to those of their Western sisters, will
we witness an increased dilution of Greek family
bonds? In fact, growing numbers of the younger
generation are joining the white-collar work

market and rising up the ranks. The secret of this transformation lies with their mothers who, after spending a lifetime bringing up their own children, are now doting over their grandchildren during the day. In rural society, women have been described by some Western-trained Greek sociologists as socially inferior. It would be hasty to go along with such a judgment without having examined the criteria involved.

Where women achieve high positions, they make a lasting impact. Bouboulina, a nineteenth-century shipping lady turned rebel, mobilized her fleet against the Turks. Melina Mercouri forcefully reintroduced the issue of the return of the Elgin Marbles (the Parthenon frieze) to Athens. The world of opera is now divided into before Maria Callas and after. Gianna Angelopoulou, a former parliamentarian, steered the nation into gaining the Olympic Games, and Dora Bacogianni, the mayor of Athens, is transforming the city.

MORE THAN LOVE

There are two forms of love in Greek. *Agápe* is the emotion of altruistic love, support, deep friendship. The feeling of parents for their child, the love of mankind for God and vice versa, the love between man and woman, husband and wife beyond the desires of the flesh. The other is *érotas.*

This is the emotion of ardent
desire between two people
motivated by erotic feelings. You
can also have *platonikós érotas,*
platonic love, where the sexual
passion is consciously avoided.
This feeling extends to *théios
érotas,* or divine love.

Like France and Italy, the sex life (or lives) of
politicians, or public personalities, does not
impact on their careers. People are not held to
ransom for their drives; that is a personal matter.

Nostalgia: A Very Greek Condition

There is a saying that Greeks suffer from two
illnesses: the first, that they want to leave Greece;
the second, that they yearn to return. This is
reflected in the large number of songs, from the
days of Homer to today's minstrels, about the
pain of *xenitiá* (having to live in foreign places).
Often, *xenitiá* is personified and asked why it took
away the beloved son, husband, friend. With a
vast *Diasporá* (meaning, scattered seeds), the pain
has traveled far, through immigrations,
deportations, exilehood, seafaring, studying. The
nearest musical equivalent may be found in
American songs about having to travel such long
distances that relationships are forever terminated
("By the time I get to Phoenix she'll be rising . . . ,"

"I'm leaving on a jet plane, don't know when I'll be back again . . ."). In the U.S.A., the "lonesome cowboys," and all their derivative lone heroes, miss their sweethearts. The Irish sing of their sweetheart, occasionally of their home county. In Greece, the loneliness caused by distance spreads the pain; the Greek misses his family, his village, his native soil, and, of course, vice versa, "Damn you *xenitiá*, you stole my boy...." "Of all the woes, *xenitiá* and orphanhood, love and sorrow, t'is *xenitiá* that carries the heaviest burden... ." "Farewell sweet Mother, good-bye Father, good-bye my siblings, and you all my cousins, I am leaving for the *xenitiá* . . ."

chapter three

CUSTOMS & TRADITIONS

HOLIDAYS AND FESTIVALS

In addition to national public holidays, different towns have their own festive holiday on the day of the town's or the island's saint protector; also particular occupations have a celebratory date. For Corfu, it is Saint Spiridon's day on December 12. On January 30 all schoolchildren have the day off in honor of Greek Letters Day and the Three Hierarchs

Main Public Holidays	
January 1	New Year
January 6	Epiphany
February (movable)	First Lent Sunday followed by Clean Monday
March 25	Greek Independence Day and Annunciation Day
April, early	May Good Friday (half day), Good Saturday, Easter Sunday, Easter Monday
May 1	Labor Day, Spring Festival
August 15	Feast of the Assumption of the Virgin
October 28	*Oxi* (pronounced *ochi*, as in "loch") Day ("No" Day)
December 25	Christmas Day
December 26	Day after Christmas Day

(St. Basil the Great, St. Gregory the Theologian, and St. John Chrysostomos). Though the Orthodox Easter usually comes after the Catholic Easter, in Greece they are both celebrated according to the Orthodox Calendar. Saint George is the patron saint of Greece, the army, shepherds, and farmers (the name George comes from *georgós*, "farmer").

TO REMEMBER: SAINTS' DAYS

Greeks whose name is also that of a saint, celebrate that day as if it were their birthday. Friends and family are expected to remember it since, though it may be impossible to remember dozens of birthdays, saints' days are always on the same day. It also avoids age references. On those days, especially outside Athens, many households that are celebrating receive a stream of guests throughout the day. Soft drinks, coffee, and cakes are offered, greetings exchanged, such as "*hrónia polá*" ("many years"). Only children receive presents. If you are eating out with a person whose name day it is, they are expected to pay. If there is no saint with your name, then your name day is on All Saints' Day, which is on the first Sunday after Pentecost. People will also call most of the people they know under that name to wish them "*hrónia polá*." So pick up your phone, too; it's a great opportunity.

Here is a list of the most popular name days. You will inevitably get to know more than one person with the following popular names:

January 1: Vasíleios, Vasílis, Vasilikí
January 7: Ioánnis, Ioánna, Yánnis, Yánna
January 17: Antónios, Andónis, Antónia
February 10: Charálambos, Hárris
February 17: Theódoros, Thódoris, Theodóra
March 25: Evángelos, Evangelía, Vangélis,
    Vangelió (Eva)
April 23: Geórgios, Yórgos, Georgía
May 5: Eiríni
May 21: Constantínos, Kóstas, Eléni
June 29: Pétros, Pávlos
July 17: Marína
July 20: Ilías
August 15: María, Marý, Mários
August 30: Aléxandros, Alexándra
October 6: Thomás
October 26: Dimítris, Dimítra
November 8: Michális, Ángelos, Angéla,
    Angelikí
November 25: Aikateríni, Kateína
November 30: Andréas
December 6: Nikólaos, Níkos, Nikoléta
December 9: Ánna
December 12: Spíros, Spiradoúla
December 25: Manólis
December 27: Stéfanos, Stefanía

THE GREEK YEAR
January 1: New Year's

This is Saint Basil's day. In Greece, it is not Santa Claus or Father Christmas who brings presents, but Hagios Vasilis (St. Basil). New Year carols, or *Kálanda*, are sung by children in the buildup to this day. You give them a few *leptá* or a euro. All housholds and most businesses, organizations, sports teams (you name it) divide the *Vassilópita* (a special New Year cake). Each person receives a slice, including slices for the household, Jesus, the poor, and the stranger. The one who receives the coin will have a lucky year (and often some money that goes with the coin). On New Year's Eve Greeks play games of chance, especially card games. Large sums of money can change hands.

January 6: *Theophánia* (Epiphany)

This is the blessing of the waters, and celebrates Christ's baptism. Throughout Greece (and in Greek communities around the world), priests bless the waters (sea, lake, river) by throwing in a cross. Young divers jump into the water and the one who retrieves it is blessed for the year.

February (movable feast): Carnival

It begins three weeks before the beginning of the Great Easter Lent. Carnival climaxes a week before the Lenten fast begins and a fifty-day fasting period. On the first Monday of Lent (*Kathará Deftéra*, Clean Monday), children take to the hilltops and fly kites. The most famous and colorful carnival is in Patras.

March 25: Independence Day, Annunciation of the Virgin

This anniversary celebrates with pomp and ceremony the day Bishop Paleon Patron Germanos raised the Greek flag of independence at the monastery of Hagia Lavra, in Kalavrita. It is also a religious festival.

April, early May: Holy Week and Easter Sunday

The Greek faith is centered on the Resurrection, so this is the most important festival in its calendar. Around 90 percent of the population attend the midnight mass on Saturday evening to celebrate the triumph of the Resurrection and the victory of light over darkness. The climax is announced with fireworks. Throughout the week, starting from Palm Sunday, a special liturgy is followed every evening marking the events leading up to the Crucifixion and the Resurrection. On Good Friday there are candle-lit processions around town led by the priests and the choir behind the *epitáphios* (a platform bearing the icon of Jesus before the Resurrection, festooned with white flowers). In the countryside they form illuminated lines in the landscape. On Saturday, at midnight, the churches go dark, and the drama heightens when suddenly the priest emerges with the light of the Resurrection, which he transmits to the congregation. It spreads, defeating the darkness of death. Immediately fireworks are set off around the country. If you can, try to attend those events, especially if you know of a good choir. On Easter Sunday, Lent fasting ends and lambs are roasted in celebration, and everyone cracks red dyed eggs.

May 1: May Day
This is a festival of spring. It is also a day when demonstrations take place asserting workers' rights—if they haven't taken to the countryside for their family picnic.

May 19: Genocide of the Pontian Greeks
In the early twentieth century up to 300,000 Pontian Greeks, in today's northeastern Turkey, were killed by the Ottoman Turks. Thousands fled to the Caucasus. In 1941 Stalin deported them to Kazakhstan and forced them to build the city of Kentau in the desert. Thousands more died.

June: Navy Week
Celebrating the nation's bond with the sea. It is accompanied by the Poseidonia, when the

shipping community from around the world gathers in Piraeus in a weeklong trade fair full of glamour, display, and classy parties.

August 15: Assumption of the Virgin

This is considered as the mini-Resurrection. On this day families get together, many of them returning to their home villages or islands. It also marks a mass exodus of vacationers. The largest pilgrimage occurs on the island of Tinos to worship a miraculous icon of the Panagía (the Virgin). Avoid traveling around this time.

September 14: Asia Minor Hellenism

In 1922, 3,000 years of Greek history in Asia Minor came to an abrupt end culminating with the burning of Smyrna.

October 28: *Óxi* ("No") Day

On this day in 1940 the Greeks, though alone, refused to give in to the Axis powers and fought to win the first Allied victory.

December 25: Christmas

This being a maritime nation, you will often see boats decorated with lights and Christmas decorations, as well as the more familiar Xmas trees. (The "X" of Xmas is the first Greek letter of the word "Christ.")

THE GREEK ORTHODOX CHURCH

Greece is the only country in the world that is officially Orthodox. When you attend the liturgy and observe ecclesiastic ritual in a Greek Orthodox Church, you are witnessing the language, sounds, gestures, and even the smells that have marked the Christian Orthodox faith of the Greeks, almost unchanged, for over a thousand years. You are witnessing the ceremony of Emperors seated at the center of their lands, and of shepherds who never ventured beyond their pastures. Elements of its rituals are pre-Christian. It is considered the mother of all Churches for a number of reasons. The Apostles and Evangelists were essentially Eastern and wrote their inspired works in the *Koiné* (common) Greek language, which is quite accessible to today's speakers. The language itself had been developing and reflecting part of mankind's daily and spiritual concerns for two thousand years before that, and was also the Apostolic tongue. Arguably, it loses much of its associations and richness when translated into English, so much so that many believe English is not ready yet for the Orthodox tradition. For instance, to translate the word *logos* as "the word," is tantamount to replacing a multicolored garden filled with melodies, with a black-and-white picture. Many Greek Christian words have passed into English—church, apostle, bible, prophet, evangelist, angel, hymn, bishop, parish, carols, tomb, coffin, heretic, atheist, idol, icon, demon . . .

The Christian faith was established through seven Councils, between 325 and 787, in the cities of Nicaea, Constantinople, Ephesus, and Chalcedonia. The Great Schism between Orthodoxy and Roman Catholicism began inadvertently over the *filioque*, the definition of the nature of the Trinity, in 589. Gradually the Roman Catholic practices developed in the West while the Orthodox refined those inherited from the Councils. After the Crusaders sacked Constantinople in 1204, it became impossible to bridge their differences.

The Icon is an integrated aspect of the faith.

The Bible is the verbal icon of Christ and the painted Icon its pictorial equivalent. The Seventh Council stipulated that both are to be venerated in the same way. The artistic value of Icons is  incidental. They are windows through which God has chosen to reveal his Kingdom, to enable mankind to discover its divine nature. There are

clear guidelines for painting an Icon. The Greek
Orthodox do not proselytize.

The Greek Orthodox Patriarchates
There are different Orthodox Patriarchates—the
Ethiopian, Russian, Finnish, Bulgarian,
Romanian, etc.—that gained their
autonomy from Constantinople and
emerged as late as 1870.
Dogmatically, there is no difference
between them, especially in the
liturgy and the Sacraments, only
variations. The Bishop of
Constantinople (who is automatically
the Patriarch) is *primus inter pares.* There are also
other Greek Orthodox Patriarchates, such as those
of Alexandria, Antioch, and Jerusalem. The last is
the guardian of the Holy Places, especially the
Tomb of the Resurrection in Jerusalem and the
Cave of the Nativity in Bethlehem; it also owns
considerable land, including that where the
Knesset stands, and many monasteries—such as
the ascetic monastery of Saint Savva in the Judean
desert, founded in 485 CE and considered the
"original university of the Christian faith."

Mount Athos, the Holy Mountain
This isolated garden of theology is the world's
only Monastic Republic, in the Halkidiki region of

northern Greece. It is ruled by twenty monasteries that look like multicolored, turreted fortresses. It is difficult to gain permission to visit it, and women have not been allowed to set foot there since its foundation in 963.

OTHER RELIGIONS
Islam
Muslims in Greece are mainstream Sunni. Islam was introduced by the Ottoman Turks and became more widespread in southeast Europe after the fall of Constantinople in 1453, often through forced conversions, though many converted for peace of mind and the privileges that went with it. Today there are around 100,000 Greek citizens who are Muslims. Most of them are in Thrace and of Turkish, Pomak, or Gypsy origin. There are still Greek Muslims in Turkey who were part of the 1923 population exchange between the two countries.

Judaism
The oldest dialogue in the world is that between Hellenism and Judaism. It is hard to imagine a world with neither Greeks nor Jews, though some have tried. There have been Jews in Greece since after Alexander the Great. Saint Paul first preached to the Jewish communities of Asia

Minor. The main influx occurred in 1496 after the expulsion of the Jews from Spain. Many headed for the port city of Thessaloniki, where they prospered. By the early twentieth century they were about half the city's total population. Greeks refer to Jews as *Hevraioi* (Hebrews), or *Ioudaioi* (Judeans).

Dodekatheists

This is not a recognized religion or one with a definite dogma and membership. A small number of Greeks have rejected the monotheistic world and adopted the long-gone faith of the Twelve Gods of Mount Olympus. Some gather in Delphi (considered of old the umbilical center of the world) and other sites and perform quirky ceremonies.

chapter four

MAKING FRIENDS

OPENNESS

Greeks are expressive rather than concise communicators. This may involve some adjustment on your behalf. If your idea of a row is witnessing people shouting and arguing in an excited manner, then you need to reexamine your expectations because in Greece this is often the standard of communication. They are not expressing aggression; they are simply involved on a more passionate level. One minute they are shouting, the next they are laughing, or parting in the nicest possible way.

In your initial stay in Greece you may feel the urge to inject some levelheadedness and lower the excitement with your calm voice. At first, people will allow you to have your say, but as the conversation picks up and your presence becomes more accepted, people will interpret your apparent calmness as meaning that you have nothing important to contribute, or as "indifference," and in the ensuing verbal cataclysm you will not be able to interject a word.

DISTINGUISH YOUR ORDERS FROM YOUR REQUESTS

If you are an English speaker, you may gain the impression that Greeks are ordering you quite bluntly to do something, such as "pass me the salt," or "bring me your papers." The thing to learn very quickly is that the Greek language, like French, German, and others, has two modes of address: the formal/polite and the informal. Formal speech is used between people who are strangers, acquaintances rather than friends, as well as toward your elders, priests, and seniors in general. It uses the plural of the second person, which is called the plural of politeness.

In the English language everyone is "you." In the absence of a polite form, especially when

requests are involved, politeness markers such as "could you," "would you," "may I," and "would you mind" are used. So if you are using the polite form in Greek and, on top of that, you add these markers you will sound absurd. Likewise, when Greeks speak English, in their minds they are transferring the polite form and so they do not use the politeness markers. As a result they can sound abrupt.

GESTURES AND PHYSICAL CONTACT

If you come from a culture where the territorial dynamics between people conversing dictate a distance of about three feet, or a meter, facing each other at right angles, you are in for a jolt. You may feel that, at just over two and a half feet (80 cm), people are crowding you. One gets used to it and it soon becomes the norm. A gay London producer who spent three days on a shoot in Athens said that for the first two days he thought that the place was full of gays, but that no one wanted to sleep with him. On the third day he realized that Mediterraneans really are more physical, compared to Anglo-Saxons, who are not at all—unless "there is something going on."

Greeks will touch your arm, hold on to your shoulder; if you are facing away, they can gently slap you on your arm to get your attention and say, "let me tell you . . ." And friends will kiss twice on the cheeks.

As for gestures and facial expressions, they are not as operatic as the Italians. These accompany speech and can be as succinct or eloquent as a thousand words. There is something sculptural about Greek gestures. Learn to read them.

WHISPERING

You will often encounter situations where your interlocutor will be gently eased away from you by someone who will quite openly talk to him confidentially. The body language is unmistakable, heads inclining, hand on the shoulder raising a protective boundary, and the hushed voice. Are they talking about you? Is something being concocted? The sense of unease is even greater in a business environment. The answer is quite harmless. More often than not, the exchange is undisruptive of your relationship. A Greek diplomat would use this tactic to say the most ordinary and inconsequential things; it simply made the receiver feel a little special and worthy.

TIMEKEEPING

At times it feels as though punctuality is illegal. Yes, people are usually late. Often there is good cause for it, especially in Athens where traffic is chaotic or officials can keep you waiting for a length of time that defies understanding. Be patient, take a book, or learn to do the same.

HOSPITALITY

The Greek word is *philoxenía*. This is a question of honor, irrespective of wealth. To attend a Greek event is to experience the meaning of plenty. A senior British official involved on the Cyprus problem so misunderstood the nature of *philoxenía* (in this case of the Greek Cypriots) that he confided to a friend that the Greeks were all very rich. He was totally, and perhaps mischievously, wrong. The notion of "beware of Greeks bearing gifts"—based on their "good-bye present" to the Trojans of a giant wooden horse filled with soldiers—is unfair. That was war.

Thousands of young and not so young tourists have enjoyed Greek hospitality, which can extend from a meal to free accommodation, or even a trip on some tycoon's yacht. Such gestures are rarely reciprocated and reciprocation is rarely expected, though doubtless they would be appreciated. Perhaps Americans, whose hospitality can be surprisingly generous, can empathize with this. The best you can offer in return is to be a good *paréa* (companion).

WHO PAYS?

When there are men and women, the man pays.
The oldest pays. At a table with many people, the
one with *kéfi* (in the grip of a well-disposed
euphoria). The one who invites. Sometimes
arguments can break out between Greeks as to
who pays; you will hear comments such as "get
back to your seat, this is mine," "I cannot accept
this, I insist this one is mine." Both men will be
waving wads of cash trying to stuff it inside the
waiter's pocket. Of course, there are times when
one person will quietly slip the money to the
waiter while no one is looking. Americans and
Australians are quite happy to join in the fray of
who pays. As for the British, well, it is not in their
culture, and the French seem to think it is owed to
them. The Italians will thank profusely and offer
eternal hospitality back home.

Nowadays, when with a group of friends,
people will increasingly go Dutch and the men
will pay for their ladies. On name days, the person
celebrating foots the bill.

GIFT GIVING

If you are invited to someone's home you should
bring a gift. Suitable presents are a box of
patisseries, flowers, chocolates, or some small
curiosity. These are generally handed to the

hostess. The gift is usually something decorative that offers temporary pleasure, unless it is for the child—a good choice. It will rarely be a CD, a book, or earthenware. If you are arriving from a village or the countryside, you can bring some local specialty. Most regions have their own; for instance, you can ask where to find the best local cheese, honey, wine, or salami. When you hand over your gift explain what it is and where it originates; it will be much appreciated. Many shops will surprise you with the exquisite bag they will provide to hold even a trivial gift.

Christmas presents in Greece are a recent import. The exchange of gifts takes place after the New Year has been sounded, or the day after if you are invited to someone's house, or, indeed, if you are having guests yourself. And of course there are birthdays, too. Another vanishing tradition is to bring gifts when you arrive from abroad. This dates to the days when Greece lacked certain goods and those who arrived were supposedly better off. But Europeanization and cheap travel have sidelined this tradition, except, to a degree, within families, when one member of the family lives permanently abroad or has been away for a while.

VISITING

When you are invited to someone's home, you will invariably be served something light to eat and drink. This can be coffee, tea, cakes, various nonalcoholic drinks, or, with the older generation "spoon sweets." The latter look like preserves, and are presented on a small plate. Everything will accompanied by water.

You do not have to dress formally, just avoid looking shabby. Casual to smart casual is fine, depending on the occasion and as long as your clothes are clean. As we have seen, often nothing is too good for the guest. You are honored and will be fussed over. As for gifts, see above. It is worth mentioning that when a Greek person is flying over to your country and you invite them to stay for a few days, they will bring you a gift. These things matter.

In typical Mediterranean style, Greeks are quite receptive to unannounced visits, be it to say "hello," for a brief chat, to inquire about the family, or just out of sheer nosiness. This is very much the norm in the countryside. Unfortunately Athens has grown a little resistant to such human interaction. In villages and more traditional urban neighborhoods, the older people will pull their chairs in front of their homes, and hold court to friends and acquaintances who happen to be walking past.

Use your discretion to judge the length of your visit. Usually blood-ties and depth of friendship allow for a longer stay. In fact, in a number of traditional Greek stories a stranger knocking on the door and dressed in rags is none other than Jesus Christ testing the hospitality of the people.

VERBAL GREETINGS: A WISH FOR LIFE

There are different forms of greeting and expressing best wishes in Greece. Appropriately enough for a nation that has experienced more than its fair share of death, most of them express wishes for life. To the parents of a newborn baby, or if you are seeing their child for the first time, you say, "*zoí na éhi*" ("may it be vigorous with life"), or, "*na sas zísi*" ("may it live for you"). Some ladies will precede such greetings with a pretend spitting sound, namely "*ftou, ftou, ftou;*" this is intended to blind the devil and avert the evil eye. On a person's birthday, a saint's name day, and during major Greek Orthodox feast days you say, "*hrónia polá*" ("many happy returns," literally "many years"). In all cases the other person will respond with the same, or "*na'ste kalá*" ("may you be well and healthy").

Even the Greek birthday song is about life and wisdom: "May you live [name of the person] and many happy returns, may you grow till your hair goes white, may you spread light across the earth, and may everyone say, here is a wise person." Then you add, "May you reach one hundred." Often, if the person is ninety-five years old, they will reply, "Why are you wishing me only five more years?!"

ALCOHOL

You will rarely see a drunken Greek—and if you do they are probably not of the Hellenic nation. The preferred high is to be in good company and build up the mood with conversation, animating the evening with stories and speculation, and making *pláka* (which is talking in a teasing manner to generate mirth). Alcohol is there more for the taste buds, to accompany the meal, or as an integral part of a dish filled with *mezé*—bite-size morsels of food such as cheese, marinated vegetables, *dolmádes*, or *keftedákia* (small meatballs). Though beware—this doesn't mean that Greeks don't drink over the limit. It is just that through their social interaction they channel their behavior well clear of the ugly conduct common in northern cultures. Driving when over the limit is far too common, and results in thousands of deaths every year. In Athens people drink wine or beer, and those in their early twenties drink bottled cocktails. In provincial towns and in the country there are also local drinks, sometimes homemade, such as *tsípouro* (made from grapes) or *rakí* (made from aniseed).

PHILÓTIMO

The world was keen to take on board the concept of philosophy. In fact, it could have done far worse than take to heart *philótimo*. This concept concerns personal honor; the ability to do something for a person above and beyond what is dictated by personal feelings or professional obligations; an ability to transcend even animosity toward that person and grant them a favor with no strings attached.

This is done when the other person needs something that only you can provide. To place yourself at the receiving end of someone's *philótimo*, you are appealing to their sense of honor, of fairplay, decency, generosity of spirit. Your appeal will not be interpreted as begging for charity because it consists of a necessary gesture between two people where there is an honest-to-god need for it. In fact, it is difficult to communicate this idea since it is specifically cultural. There is also an art in triggering someone's *philótimo*; for instance, in getting your unreliable builder to finish that job today because of the dire consequences to yourself, or of getting out of a fine, avoiding penalization, you name it. Any slackening of this wonderful institution is a sure sign that the nation's sense of personal honor and self-esteem is in decline.

chapter five

DAILY LIFE

TOWN AND COUNTRY

Aristotle described civilized man as "by nature an animal of the *polis*." Civilization was born in city-states and Greeks almost instinctively move to cities. After the Second World War many fled to Athens and Thessaloniki to avoid famine, the civil war, and the accompanying banditry. Unfortunately, since those days, officials also forgot the words "town-planning." Much of Athens was transformed from one of the world's most pleasant cities in the 1950s to a concrete maze. The *coup de grâce* came from the law of *antiparochí* ("in exchange for"). It allows the owners of a plot of land or of a pleasant house with its garden to hand it to a developer. The latter levels the place and builds a concrete apartment block on the site. The original owner is then handed a percentage of the apartments, which he sells or rents out. The buildings are built back-to-back and there are hundreds of thousands of windows whose view is a concrete wall seven feet (two meters) from your nose, literally. Under the PASOK government, matters became worse. Greece was introduced for the first time to easy credit. On top of that, a planning law enabled developers to sell their unused height to someone else. The result is that in the narrow streets of central Athens there is a new explosion of seven- and eight-story buildings going up at an alarming rate, dwarfing most of the remaining neoclassical architecture.

So this leaves the countryside. The law of *antiparochí* applies there, too, but the pace is not so frenetic and life can be sweet; however, there is no convenient network of trains for commuting to develop.

WATER—A VANISHING COMMODITY

For a Mediterranean people, the Greeks are surprisingly wasteful of water. The good visitor should be water-conscious. Indeed, there are two things to observe about this commodity. It is scarce,

and too many Greeks disregard this fact. Toilets
are flushed repeatedly and at full strength, dishes
are washed with faucets full on. Thousands of
households and hundreds of communities even
waste it on grass lawns, to achieve that "northern
look." In some parts of the country the European
Union goes as far as demanding cultivation of
water-thirsty crops. But you, the foreign visitor or
resident, can act responsibly. Turn on the shower
only when you need the water. Have a bucket handy
so that when you are waiting for the water from the
faucet or shower to turn from cold to hot you can
intercept the potential wastage and use it for the
toilet, or to soak some clothes, to water the plants,
or to wash your balcony. And when you are told,
anywhere in the country, that there is plenty of
water, this is sheer ignorance talking.

THE (UN)CIVIL SERVANT MENTALITY
One afternoon, a Greek minister paid a surprise
visit to a public utility office. The place was
empty. He asked the superintendent, "Doesn't
anyone work in the place?" The answer was,
"Minister, they don't work in the morning; in the
afternoon they simply don't turn up." The name
of the enemy is *demósios ypálilos*, the public
servant. Through them you will experience a form
of bureaucratic fascism. You must avoid their

vengefulness, so keep calm. One longtimer in Athens recommends that if you have to lose your temper, then go ballistic. There is no mechanism to take up your grievance and no one who would risk taking action to remedy it. So, do you really want to report serious damage done to your residence by cowboy builders? Do you actually want to pay some bureaucratic bill? You arrive and there is no one at the department entrance to give you directions. Then you see people going up and down the stairs—the elevator probably does not work—from one office to the other. The officials give you conflicting advice, revealing ignorance and lack of interest. Soon you join those poor people going up and down the stairs and begin to feel as though you are caught in an Escher engraving. You can spend hours, if not days, in this rut. But don't miss the poster on the wall praising the competence of the administration. Also, observe that only one in five desks has a computer terminal, useful for playing solitaire by bored employees. Shortcuts can only be found through friends and family with relevant connections, or if there is any *philótimo* left in your torturers.

The Eternal Problem
"The public sector has never been for the average Greek an area which could seriously claim his

loyalty and with which he could identify.
Corporate loyalty outside the family has been as
rare as a sense of security outside the same social
unit. Modern Greeks entered the civil service as
marauding invaders in enemy territory: to
plunder, pillage and bring the spoils back to the
haven of the family." This passage comes from
Greece—The Modern Sequel, by J. S. Koliopoulos
and T. M. Veremis.

EDUCATION

Across the millennia, Greeks of all classes have
prized education, opening schools, if not
academies, wherever they have settled. Alexander
the Great did it, the Orthodox Church continues
the tradition, and so does the modern Greek
state. In Greece proper, kindergarten begins at
five. Primary school is from ages six to twelve. It
is followed by six years of High
School (divided between
Gymnásium, followed by
Lýkio). Education is
obligatory up to
sixteen. A very high
proportion of young
people go to
university, which in Greece is free. Around
40,000 Greeks continue their further or

postgraduate studies abroad—over half in Britain, the rest in the U.S.A., France, Germany, and Italy, and also in Hungary, Romania, Bulgaria, and Poland. Greece has one of the highest percentages of its student population studying abroad. One reason is that traditionally, especially under the (anti-education) Ottoman Turks, parents who could afford it, or who found patrons, would send their progeny abroad to study. The other reasons are fashion and the lack of university places in Greece.

Military service is compulsory for all young men at eighteen, and lasts for one year. For those entering further education, it is deferred until after graduation.

WORK
People rise early, at around 6:00–6:30 a.m. Because simple tasks can take ages to accomplish, it is best to follow suit. On weekends, offices remain shut. Work, or *douleiá*, is a mixed blessing; it still bears, just slightly, its original meaning of slavery, or heavy, obligatory, and unrewarding work. Its other translation, *ergasía*, on the other hand, still refers to the involvement of mind and body for the accomplishment of a task. So a "working lunch," should be a *gévma ergasías*, not a *gévma douleiás*.

OPENING HOURS

Opening hours vary according to the day of the week, the week of the year, the seasons, whether it is in Athens or not, depending on the feast days. Weekends add their own twist.

As a rule, shops open after 9:00 a.m. and close from 2:00 p.m. onward; they reopen at 5:00 p.m. until 8:00 p.m. All shops are closed on Saturday afternoons and Sundays. Government offices open between 7:00 and 7:30 a.m., banks between 8:00 a.m. and 2:00 p.m., and post offices between 7:30 a.m and 2:00 p.m. In major cities some stay open until 8:00 p.m. Pharmacies advertise their opening hours; if closed, there will be a notice informing you where to find one open.

In the summer the heat changes the timetables. In August many premises are closed, especially in towns, with their owners off on vacation or to their village. For those small commodities, from newspapers to dry snacks, you will find a *períptero* (kiosk) open most hours. The long and short of it is that once you have located your stomping ground, ask what the opening hours are.

SIESTA LAW

Ahh, siesta; that civilizing institution that relaxes your body and adds longevity to your years. Of course, the Greeks have siesta time. Only, they

don't have a word for it—not even "siesta." It is imperative to know that between 3:00 p.m. and 6:00 p.m. you do not call people at home; they are probably taking a nap. It is fully recommended that you do the same, especially during the hot season. For those working in offices, siesta time can occur between 5:00 p.m. and 7:00 p.m.

FINDING A PLACE TO LIVE

If you intend to stay for longer than a couple of months, it will be cheaper and more rewarding to rent an apartment. The procedure is quite straightforward and is usually preceded by a written rental agreement (the usual caution applies). Learn what your responsibilities and rights are. Quite often the agreement is oral, with no contract, and the rent is paid in cash. As for the quality, just think of your student days back home. Your employers or friends can be mobilized to find you something suitable. It is also quite acceptable to ask at kiosks or local shops if they know of suitable places. Always view the premises beforehand, if only to find out the level of furnishing.

If you intend to stay for a considerable length of time (over six months), inspect your preferred areas of residence late at night. If you see cars parked bumper-to-bumper, it means that, if you have a car, it will be a problem to find a parking space within a wide radius. If you have a family, especially with small children, take note as to whether cars are parked on the sidewalk. In cities, many sidewalks are nothing more than obstacle courses of cars, trash cans, motorbikes, and rubble, repeatedly forcing you to walk in the busy streets. Imagine having to dive in and out of traffic with a child and your shopping.

ECONOMIC PRIORITIES

A sure sign of the Greek love of creature comforts and the fear of having to make do with less is the collapse of the country's birthrate. One Athenian sociologist called it "the empty cradle of democracy." Whereas their parents and grandparents considered it a blessing to have several children, modern Greeks barely have one child. The new generation may have to pay the price in a lonely old age. One successful lady in her forties confessed that she and her husband had first wanted to enjoy traveling, then they needed their own apartment, then a smaller one outside Athens, better cars, and more time going out with their friends. Time passed, and then it was too late to have children.

During economic downturns Greeks will cut out foreign travel. Recently they have cut back on going out to restaurants—something they would normally do several times a week.

BANKING AND PAYMENTS

Greece just about offers the banking services of the average EU member state. Credit cards are widely used, with a large section of society preferring cash transactions. Always take ID to the bank, and be prepared to wait. Some shops give 10 percent discount for cash. Greece has adopted the euro, so there is no need to change money if you are arriving from the eurozone. All cities and small towns have banks, most of them with ATMs. Currency-exchange bureaus are widely available; in any case, you may readily find someone who will accept your U.S. dollars or British pounds and give you change in euros.

In a bank you may occasionally notice the manager or the bank clerk obviously engaged in a conversation or activities unrelated to their duties. Unless time is desperately short, let it pass. Otherwise you may attempt to trigger their sense of *philótimo* with your particular circumstances to speed up procedures.

Battling Against Corruption
Greece is plagued with it, but slowly fighting back.
In 2000 the passenger ferry *Express Samina* sank
off the island of Paros with the loss of eighty-two
passengers. It appears that inspectors pocketed a
bribe to sign papers of certification. The owners,
Minoan Lines, were accused of operating like
cowboy businessmen. Certainly, the company was
not family-based and lacked the consciousness of
family shipping enterprises. In 2004, the merchant
marine disciplinary council permanently revoked
the professional crew licenses of the three senior
officers of the *Express Samina*. The captain and
Minoan Lines officials are facing criminal charges
for multiple counts of murder with possible
premeditated malice, endangering maritime
transportation, endangering passengers, and
causing a shipwreck.

SHIPPING

Shipping is ideal in demonstrating how the
Greeks work at their best; it combines family, sea,
and mistrust of authority. The Greeks dominate
tramp shipping, which involves crossing the seven
seas according to whichever way the trade winds
blow. This means that each trip, each contract, is
negotiated separately. There are international

maritime rules regulating these matters, but each port has its own specifications, each country its own requisites. Now take liner shipping. This involves a company working a line of ships crossing between the same ports for most of their seaworthy lives. Everything is settled, regulated, predictable, dependent on the strict laws of the countries involved. With tramp shipping, no one country can pin down the company. One port closes, another opens. One country is out of bounds, another will pick up its cargo. Vast populations need to eat, build, export, import. Ships are their bloodline.

To undertake this vast commitment you need reliable personnel, experienced, with an almost instinctive understanding of the particularities of the different nations under the sun. Shipping companies will usually expand as far as the extended family connections will allow them, though their international maritime network circles the globe. The companies do not go public—it would be like involving strangers in family affairs. Besides, what impersonal institution with its nine-to-five rhythms can maintain the round-the-clock attention required by global shipping? Master Mariner Vyron

Michaelides said it succinctly (reinterpreted from shipping historian Gelina Harlaftis):

"The famous genius at sea is something beyond any rules or rationalization. It is something like what Zorba the Greek says: 'I cannot explain it with words, so I will explain it with dancing.' It is sailing against the mainstream. It is the exploitation of certain opportunities in critical periods in shipping. It is to buy when others sell. To sail when others lay up, to order the building of new ships when others don't even dream of it. It is the deep belief of the Greek that the sea becomes ill but she never dies."

PRICES

Prices are stable, but the cost of living is ineluctably increasing, especially since the introduction of the euro. Greece is always a paradise, but no longer a budget paradise. In many places in central Athens the price of coffee, soft, and alcoholic drinks can easily surpass those of central Manhattan. Likewise for clubbing, concerts, and CDs, which are often more expensive than in most Western European capitals. Prices for certain food items (lamb, turkey, fish) can increase temporarily in the run-up to important religious festivals. What the country excels at is allowing you to spend hours

sitting in a beautiful, shaded spot, sipping your
drink, reading your book, or talking away.

STANDARDS OF LIVING

Welcome to the paradox of Hellenic life.
According to statistics, Greece was the poorest of
the fifteen countries in the EU, as it stood before
the May 2004 enlargement (though in the top
thirty worldwide). Now look again. People seem
more comfortable than in many
European countries,
including Britain. What
are we missing? Quite a
bit. The family support
system means that often
everyone chips in to help
out. It is not uncommon

for people in their thirties to live in their
parents' house. Then we have the shadow
economy that is there for everyone to see. It is
difficult for the state to monitor the self-
employed, including doctors, landlords, and
tradesmen. There is also the retail industry, where
many exchanges go unregistered. In fact, there are
so many small- to medium-sized enterprises,
coupled with the state's policy of recruiting on
the grounds of personal connections rather
than job suitability, that any statistics fail to

show the real picture—perhaps by a wide margin.

One must also bear in mind the Greek penchant for enjoying life. A sixteenth-century Greek proverb (though it reads more like a song) said, "Like a Greek at table, like a Greek at sea, as good as a Greek at night in the sack, like a Greek with the sword."

A Land for Living

You may wonder what is the point of settling for a length of time in Greece. The same question was asked of a New York Greek woman who had left her promising career at the UN headquarters to live in Greece. Her original motivation had been love, and though the engagement did not last she found a relatively rewarding job in Athens. She soon discovered that career advancement was not a Greek term, to say the least. But the lifestyle kept here there. She explained how, two weekends previously, she and three friends had flown to Ioannina for a weekend, to stay at a mountain inn. At night it snowed heavily, and they spent part of it dancing in the blizzard as their hosts played the *toumbeléki* (local percussive instruments). On their return, the flight was canceled and they experienced a riotous, eight-hour bus journey to Athens. The weekend after, they were swimming in a lake.

FOR RICHER, FOR POORER

There is, of course, poverty in Greece. There are
people living in damp basements or in small, dark
apartments, with no access to green spaces and
subsisting on an unhealthy diet of carbohydrates.
There is also extreme wealth—of the *nouveau riche*
variety. Some of this has been generated by EU
funds ending up in private pockets. Other sources
of money have come in the form of lucrative
government contracts that for some reason simply
end up restoring a few buildings and paying for
the publication of glossy brochures. This
phenomenon became a marked characteristic of
the PASOK government, something it is now
trying to live down. Perhaps the greatest tragedy
rests in the inability of the Greek state to absorb its
brightest talents. They move abroad, though the
success of the Athens Olympic Games seems to be
slowly tilting the country toward recognizing the
necessity of meritocracy.

But for the thousands of immigrants, life is
getting sweeter by the day. They are learning new
skills, their children are enjoying free education,
and many move on to a free university education.
The best of them are often picked off by U.S.
institutions. Their remittances provide a welcome
income to their home country.

TIME OUT

TAVERNAS, RESTAURANTS, AND COFFEE-HOUSES

A sure sign of a civic society is the variety of opportunities it offers to satisfy the needs of the population. One cannot underestimate the Greek skill in running welcoming premises where people can assuage their hunger for both food and conversation. Coffee was first introduced to England in 1648 by a Cretan, Bishop Conopios of Samos, when a student at Oxford; the first coffeehouse (*kafeneíon*) in London was opened by Paschalis Rosée; their compatriots opened many others. The art of running coffeehouses where people drank the hot beverage, kept awake, and debated (as opposed to drank alcohol, fought, and passed out) provided a major platform in the intellectual revolution that took place in England and the rise of newspapers (coffee sharpens your focus on the world, beer blurs it). In Greece, the *kafeneíon* is still a dignified male preserve. Inside, the lights are harsh, facilities and decoration are Spartan. The tables spill outside, especially in central squares around the country, and men who are past their flush of youth sit talking politics, local affairs, playing cards, *távli* (backgammon), flicking their *kombolói*, and sipping coffee. As a (foreign) woman, you will be treated courteously. This male preserve does not have to prove itself with heavy alcohol consumption or with displays of macho manhood.

Tavernas are for eating and drinking. You can even inspect the food. They are the working person's eatery, irrespective of status; a place you can treat as your lunchtime canteen. Sometimes they only open in the evening, in which case they become extensions of people's living rooms, a place to be expansive. The atmosphere has probably remained the same since antiquity.

Restaurants (*estiatorío*) offer a more continental European style of cuisine, but also Greek dishes. They are mostly found in central urban areas, and tend to be more expensive.

On Saturday evening or Sunday lunch, families and couples often eat out. They prefer the informal environment of the taverna, especially if it has a garden; children can run around and people can be a little more expansive.

Oh yes, there is also the *souvlatzídiko*, better known for serving gyros and kebabs to go, though many have tables. And we must not forget the *fastfoudádika*—you may discern the words "fast food." If you cannot do without your daily hamburger, this is the place for you. So "*kali órexi*," bon appétit!

TIPPING

Service is usually included, and tips are not expected. If you are particularly pleased with the service, you can leave some loose change, which will be much appreciated.

The *zaharoplasteíon* is equivalent to the French patisserie: glass shelves are filled with cakes, and the air oozes with calories. Many have tables, which make them ideal places to treat the children, or perfect for august ladies to delve into the secrets of their social life. You may notice that where men sit together, they face the world, surveying. Women, on the other hand, tend to close around into a circle.

KOUVENDOÚLA: THE ART OF IDLE TALK

Greeks enjoy their *kouvendoúla*—idle chitchat about everything and nothing, finding out about each other, and gossiping about their world, which is a sure way of making it more familiar and reassuring. As for politics, it is part of the daily discourse. If you enjoy a good debate, if you have always wanted to thrash out your ideas about world events or major developments in history, you are in the right country.

SMOKING

A nonsmoking admirer of Greece was once asked why he visited the place so often. He replied that he had become addicted to passive smoking. Greeks don't simply smoke; they are among the heaviest smokers in the world. Until recently, they came third after China and Cuba. Today they are in the top ten. They pay a heavy price in the ever-increasing levels of lung cancer and other respiratory diseases.

SHOPPING

Greek shops offer a full range of goods. If you are a connoisseur of window-shopping go to Kolonáki, in central Athens, or most other chic districts, where you will encounter exquisite small boutiques specializing in temptation. There are also entire streets dedicated to bargain clothing, leather goods, and, outside Athens, rows of glass buildings filled with lights. Greek specialties are imaginative earthenware, icons, silverware, shoes, and furs in Macedonia. If you travel around the country, keep your ears pricked and your taste buds moist for special delicacies such as local wines, *tsípouro*, salami, cheese, olive oil, yogurt, honey, or preserves.

THEATER AND CINEMA

Greeks love theater and the cinema. There are hundreds of professional and amateur companies performing everything from Euripides, to Ibsen, to the works of modern Greek playwrights. Greece is unique in offering ancient plays in their original theaters, many with a natural  backdrop of the sea and up to 2,500 years old, especially at Epidaurus and Herodus Aticus under the Parthenon.

The international reputation of Greek cinema is centered on the works of Theo Angelopoulos and Michalis Cacoyannis. The first Greek feature film was produced in 1914, based on the (still) famous play *Golfo* that was originally written and performed in Akrata. The golden age of Greek cinema was between the 1950s and early 1970s, when hundreds of films were shot. Though the melodramas, invariably involving misunderstandings and broken hearts, were soon forgotten, the comedies are still avidly watched today on TV screens and purchased on DVDs. They are quintessentially Greek, and often the actors would improvise their lines. Most of them include a couple of popular hit songs. The French TV channel Canal+ once used selected extracts from those films to re-create Athens before its concrete entombment. Greek cinema did not explore social realism like neighboring Italy, probably due to the political situation in the country.

The annual Thessaloniki Film Festival is gaining a worldwide reputation, especially for films from the broader southeastern European region.

MUSEUMS

Museums in Greece focus on archaeology, though in Athens and Thessaloniki you will find key museums on Byzantine art and iconography.

The National Archaeological Museum

This is one of the richest ancient Greek art museums in the world and the most important archaeological museum in Greece. A must for all visitors to Athens.

The National Art Gallery and Alexandros Soutzos Museum

This unique collection in Athens is devoted to the history of Greek and Western European art. It mounts superb exhibitions.

Benaki Museum

A fine example of gifts to the nation by wealthy, usually expatriate, benefactors, this neoclassical mansion was the home of the Benaki family. They were Alexandrian Greeks who prospered during the days when Greeks and Anglo-Greeks controlled up to one-third of the British cotton trade. It was donated with its ever-growing collection in 1931. It exhibits Greek material, art, and relics. Its cafeteria is a heaven above the Athenian fray, overlooking Zappeion Park—another donation by a wealthy trader, Mr. Zappas.

Vrellis Museum

Seven and a half miles (12 km) south of Ioannina, this museum has wax models of characters from the Ottoman period and the Greek War of Independence. The building is a fortress-style urban structure of the eighteenth century.

The Merchant Maritime Museum

Situated in Piraeus, this museum captures 3,000 years of shipping and houses a library.

The Lefkos Pyrgos (the White Tower)
Situated on the Thessaloniki waterfront, this
fifteenth-century defensive structure houses
collections of medieval art objects in its
winding galleries.

As for the city, Thessaloniki curves around the
Thermaikos bay and offers many examples of
Roman, Byzantine, and Ottoman architecture. It
can only be described as the younger sister of
Rome and Constantinople/Istanbul.

ARCHAEOLOGICAL SITES

The entire country seems to be parceled up into
excavated and unexcavated archaeological sites.
Dig and ye shall find. Certainly any
museum worth its salt has findings
from Greece. The question
is, where do you draw the
line between preserving
the past and getting on
with life? Few people
realize that the entire land is
divided into archaeological regions with their
regional directorates. The relevant official has
only to mark out an area as an archaeological site
and everything stops; you cannot build on it or
cultivate it. It will remain idle for decades until
the archaeologists decide what to do. Not

surprisingly, thousands of sites and ancient objects have been destroyed by private landowners fearing the "neutralization" of their property by such crude laws.

THE PARTHENON

The Parthenon was made possible by the leadership of an inspired head of state and heir to a shipping fortune, Pericles. It is an integrated architectural marvel, 2,500 years old, more a symphony of divine proportions than a manmade structure, the product of subtle mathematics, crowned by sculptured friezes supporting the roof that still shimmer in the light. In about 1580, the Peloponnesian author and historian Theódoros Zygomalas extolled to his German correspondent the beauty of the Parthenon and "the sculptures all around it showing the history of the Greeks." Subsequent invaders, some with savage instincts, respected its integrity— except for Lord Elgin who regarded key structural elements of the building as desirable independent sculptures and removed them in 1801.

Perhaps the most exquisite, most harmonious building on the Acropolis (and in the world?) is the Erechtheion. According to ancient mythology, that is where the original inhabitants were called to choose the name of their city. Athena, the goddess of wisdom, struck the ground and made a gift of the olive tree. Poseidon offered them splendid war horses. The locals chose wisdom and the tree, and named their city after Athena.

CHURCHES AND MONASTERIES

The Greek tourist office publicity machine is missing out on the country's Byzantine heritage. After all, St. Paul crisscrossed these lands and preached under the Acropolis. Perhaps this oversight is due to the fact that religion is an integral part of people's lives. Having throngs of tourists with their twirling tour guides ambling through your church is disruptive. Perhaps, unlike Italian churches, there are no easily identifiable great masters to whom Westerners can feel their art is umbilically linked. As one Greek Orthodox archimandrite pointed out, Orthodoxy is more the Christianity of the heart than of logic; no matter how much Western visitors wish to escape from their daily lives, they prefer parting from their logic only when inebriated, dancing to the rhythms of the *bouzoúki*, not in a quiet space formulated by thousands of years of theology. But do not readily expect to encounter a walking, talking spiritual encyclopedia on Orthodoxy. The Greeks have no skills or interest in proselytizing. You are baptized at birth and that is it; there is no "born again" choice. In a way, Orthodoxy works by seduction; the liturgy is (or should be) melodious, the incense uplifting, the sacramental wine sweet, the icons stirring.

So this brings us to the monasteries. Some are impregnable fortresses, as at Meteora; all are withdrawn from the world. This does not mean they are holier-than-thou. The late Father Paisios, a monk and a landmark in theology, told a group of wide-eyed schoolboys on a pilgrimage to Mount Athos, "If you are a fly [allegorically speaking], then you will avoid all the flowers and find a piece of excrement to land on, even in such a Holy mountain." Since the 1990s there has been a marked increase in the number of convents, initiated by young women who have renovated entire abandoned monasteries. Monastic produce is often quite appealing to the senses. Dress appropriately: long skirt or trousers, arms covered.

A number of religious establishments house miraculous icons, or even preserve the body of their saint protector. Some attract pilgrims, like the Panagia of the island of Tinos, which draws huge numbers of physically impaired persons and others seeking divine intercession, on August 15.

A more unusual religious festival takes place on May 21, the feast day of Saints Constantine and Helen, the *Anastenária*, at Langadas, outside Thessaloniki. After a couple of days of rhythmic chanting, people walk, unscathed, on burning embers as an expression of their faith.

OPEN MARKETS

Street markets are a feast for all the senses, including one's sense of drama. Across Greece certain streets will hold their weekly or biweekly vegetable market. All other business closes down and the streets fill up with seasonal produce. The entire neighborhood seems to converge on the stalls as people pick and choose what they would like to cook over the next few days. Local producers can be quite proud of their goods and will advertise them as such.

THE *EXOHIKÓ*—THE ANCESTRAL/COUNTRY HOME

Until the 1970s Greece was an agricultural country. With the massive exodus to cities, mostly to Athens, people left behind them their ancestral homes. Today, many Greeks retain the connection and will spend some part of the year there. Up to half a million Athenians are even registered on the electoral roll of their village or island and, if only for this, return there for a day to vote. Usually, those homes are not for sale. Links to villages can stretch back hundreds of years, but Greeks are not really awed by such pedigrees.

If you buy a country home, it is called an *exohikó*. It can be a few hours' drive away from Athens and easily accessible for weekends. Greece being so beautiful, most Greeks prefer to vacation in their own country perhaps taking a short trip abroad every few years.

But why buy? Average prices for renting a place by the year can be very reasonable. It is well worth investigating, and you can even let your friends use it. Electricity and local property taxes are extra.

SPORTS

The increasing successes of Greeks at athletics and other international sporting events are indicative of their love of sports. They regularly reach the quarterfinals (if not the finals) at basketball, volleyball, and often dominate Greco-Roman wrestling and weight lifting. They also play water polo, enjoy diving, snorkeling, and windsurfing.

The favorite competitive sport is football (soccer). Faithful to the native ability to surprise the entire world, the Greek national team won the

Euro 2004 football championship—a rank outsider, it defeated the favorites, the hosts, and the reigning champions.

Greece offers the sports enthusiast everything from skiing to hiking, mountaineering, diving, and sailing. The fact that most outsiders are totally unaware of these possibilities has more to do with marketing than the reality on the ground. Rugby and American football are not for them. Corfu has its own cricket league.

THE OLYMPIC GAMES

In 2004, the Olympics returned home. Greece was the smallest country to hold the modern Olympic Games and, according to the International Olympic Committee, they were the most successful ever, held in the most modern and welcoming stadiums and sports facilities built for the occasion. They witnessed the largest participation of countries (202), athletes, volunteers, and worldwide audiences, and, incidentally, the largest distribution of free condoms to the athletes.

Despite all the security fears of holding the world's largest event after 9/11, the police reported only twenty incidents, most of them minor. Meanwhile the international media, after an initial and fruitless hunt for hard-hitting stories, gave up and ended up congratulating the country. Many even thanked the Greeks and apologized, in Greek, for their initial doubts. The country also successfully launched a parallel "cultural Olympiad" during the Games. It also succeeded in commiting the UN and world leaders into supporting a truce during the Games in the future. This has yet to be implemented but the impetus is now truly there.

Inevitably, there were some scandals, namely concerning doping. Two of the country's world track and field champions and their trainer ran an absurd "marathon" of excuses to avoid being tested. Greece vowed to initiate a worldwide campaign against doping in sports. Greek people were reminded of the value of *athlitismós* (athletics) as a beneficial activity for mind and body, as opposed to *protathlitismós* (athletics as an obsessive drive to be *protos*, first, at all costs).

Perhaps the most exhilarating events, impossible to repeat anywhere else, were the running of the Marathon along its ancient route, and the return of the Games to their original site, after 1,411 years, with the holding of the Shot Putting contest in the ancient Olympic stadium at Olympia. Only this time women were allowed, both as spectators and as participants. The poignancy of the moment was expressed by Stavros Sklavos, an FBI-trained police officer in charge of security at the government's information and press center in Zappeion Park, in Athens. A tall, tough, stern man, he originates from a village near Olympia. On duty and unable to attend the event, this apparently flinty officer became momentarily tearful as he described his respect for his land and his pain at not being able to attend the return of the Games to the landscape  of his childhood. Likewise, Greek Defense Minister Spilios Spiliotopoulos, who attended this return, commented to his entourage that he literally felt the ground tremble beneath his feet as he walked through the arch and into the stadium that had greeted those ancient spectators centuries before. Of course, the moment was unforgettable for all those from around the globe who were lucky enough to be present.

A key question concerns the cost of the event, which rose to 7 billion euros, including 1.2 billion euros on security. The government, perhaps over-optimistically, explained that much of this can be seen as investment in modern infrastructure, and so as an investment in the future of the country and the region at large.

chapter seven

TRAVEL, HEALTH, AND SECURITY

Mainland Greece is extremely mountainous. This presented the country with the near-impossible challenge of developing a comprehensive road and rail network. Traveling east to west still involves wide detours, but new expressways, tunnels, and bridges are gradually reducing the obstacles.

BUSES

Greece is linked by buses, from the ports of disembarkation to the goat villages. They are operated by KTEL (Intercity Road Transport Companies, but just ask for the KTEL station). Turn up half an hour beforehand to buy your ticket, which will allot you a numbered seat. Today all buses are air-conditioned; so a word of warning: the downside of air-conditioning, globally, is that it can overheat or chill the air. It also targets different parts of your body, drilling into it with various consequences. The DIY response is to use a strategically placed small towel on the exposed part of your body, or over the wind vent, to keep your ethereal tormentor at bay.

TAXIS

Greek taxi drivers behave like taxi drivers everywhere, and that, generally speaking, is not a compliment. Otherwise, if you can speak the language, know where you're going, and like short blasts of conversation with no follow-ups, you will find them amenable and a fount of information. There is one thing you should understand immediately: even if it already has a passenger, a taxi will pick up others along the way, if they are heading in the direction of the first passenger. Bystanders will be flagging down taxis that are visibly engaged, shouting their destination to the driver. Occasionally, you too will have to shout your destination. Don't be shy; that gets you nowhere. At certain hours of the day few empties will stop—they are either on call or racing back to base for the change of shift.

There are two tariffs. From 6:00 a.m. to midnight the tariff should be on the day rate (tariff 1); it goes up after that (tariff 2). By law, prices and extras should be displayed on the front passenger seat in Greek and English. "Bonuses" are added during public holiday periods, and there is a small surcharge for luggage and journeys to the airport.

TRAINS—A SECRET WORLD

Welcome to another well-kept secret: Greece by rail. Visually, it is the closest you will get to flying without leaving the ground. It will take you along gorges, cling onto the sides of mountains with sheer drops to the plains below, curve around passes where not even a Pindus mule would venture. You will sail along the shoreline, or hover high with the seagulls. Your travel companions will depend on your choice of service. If you have the slightest desire to escape, there will be stops in the middle of nowhere of such pristine beauty that you half expect to meet the inhabitants of days gone by. In Thrace you can even cross bear country.

There are two levels of rail service. The old-timers are slow trains with rickety carriages. They

 fill up with soldiers heading for the frontier, migrants, students, and poor villagers traveling to or from their sons and daughters in the large cities. They are a step back in

time, with bursts of lively conversation, live music, and stiff backs. They are best avoided, unless you take them as hop-overs between villages. The other service is the intercity from Athens to Alexandroupolis, or along the narrower gauge lines to the Peloponnese. Just sit and watch the world go by—and pick out the areas you would like to return to.

THE METRO AND TRAMS

Athens has a brand-new metro. It is clean and avoids the choking traffic. However, being a late addition in an overcrowded city, most stops seem to be situated in the middle of nowhere. But this being Athens, much of the tunneling  has been dug through three thousand years of history; the upside is that a number of stations have been transformed, literally, into mini archaeological museums.

The original Athens tram was ripped up in 1960 to give the city a more Westernized look. Then came the explosion of concrete blocks and the city began turning into a charmless maze of gray apartments. Now the tram is back again, spanking new since it began operating in 2004.

BOATS

Greece without boats would be like a fish without a tail. The Greek word for trade, *embório*, was determined by the geography of this impossibly mountainous, water-dependent land. The act of passing from one shore to the other was called *póros*. The person who carried out such activities was the trader with his goods; he was the one crossing, the *émboras*. From this we eventually received the word "emporium." We also derived from it the word "porn." Today a myriad ferries, hydrofoils, taxi boats, yachts, and sailing boats link the galaxy of islands across the Greek waters. Traveling time varies considerably and the trade picks up in April–October. Some unprofitable routes are lifelines to the inhabitants of several islands. Book your crossings in advance. Depending on the class you choose to travel and the quality of the ship, you will encounter anything from all to none of the challenges of mass travel. The view of endless islands and islets slowly zooming in and out of view in that mythical light will ease most discomforts. You will not hear of disappointments.

CARS: A HEALTH WARNING

Cars are easy to rent, but expensive compared to
other European countries. They are worth
investing in occasionally for getting out of Athens
or exploring wider regions, though you should
make absolutely certain that your insurance
covers you! If not, forget it. Greece has the worst
road fatality and accident rate in Europe. In the
last ten years over 20,000 people have died on the
roads; more than 43,000 over the last twenty
years. During the main holiday weekends, up to
fifty people perish. Those small altars on the sides
of the roads commemorate loved ones who were
killed on the spot. The greatest fault lies with
drivers passing, and with the condition of
many roads. Even though you may be
driving defensively you will find it
impossible to maintain a safe distance
between yourself and the car in front
of you, because there is always some
driver passing dangerously and filling in the gap.
Admittedly, things are improving.

Motorbikes are responsible for most accidents
involving tourists.

WALKING

Greeks, especially city-dwellers, are reluctant to
walk for over five minutes. Often this can mean

that the countryside belongs to you, if you are the walking type. Even relaxing by the sea, they would rather take the car for a loaf of bread than walk for a few minutes.

HEALTH

This is a healthy state, with higher than average levels of hypochondria. These can often clog hospitals during an average flu epidemic. Take with you all relevant national and private health insurance documents and forms. If you are an EU citizen, you are guaranteed a level of care, but take those documents (and photocopy them). For a lengthy stay, clear those details *before* you leave. If not, call your embassy for information. Also, register with the IKA (pronounced "eeka") scheme, the Greek national health system. Overall, Greek doctors are highly competent, though there is a lack of specialists and emergency practitioners. They tend to prescribe antibiotics at the drop of a hat; you can even buy them over the counter. Avoid them unless there is something serious. Usually friends will direct you to someone they know. Dentists are efficient and affordable. Make sure your practitioners are IKA-registered. Medical facilities become sparse outside the major cities. Nursing care may be less than adequate, most of it being taken up by relatives.

For those who do not speak Greek, you can call the toll-free number 112 if in need of emergency services. Callers will be able to receive information and make emergency requests in English and French.

Clothing

Greece has four seasons. That should make it clear what type of clothes you need. Athens can get very chilly in the winter, and is boiling hot in the summer. Don't forget your hat. The Greeks dress "smart casual," and also like to be formal—you are what you wear.

SECURITY

Greece is one of the safest countries in the world. It remains so even with the crime rate rising, especially with the arrival of hundreds of thousands of immigrants. According to the police, the rise is mostly due to Albanian activity, though most are law-abiding citizens. The murder rate is around one in a million, and most are domestically related or crimes of passion. However, the emergence of burglary-related murders is, again, linked to Albanian perpetrators; this was not a Greek phenomenon.

chapter eight

BUSINESS
BRIEFING

THE GREEK ECONOMY

Greece has the most advanced economy in the region, with a deeply rooted business culture. It emerged from the Second World War and the ensuing civil war totally ruined. Then its economic performance grew steadily from the 1950s and took a remarkable leap in the 1990s with vast infrastructure projects. Unprecedented fiscal and monetary discipline led to rapid disinflation and improvement in public finances.

The result was macro-economic stability and real convergence with its EU partners. The government deficit remains high. Greece joined the EU in 1981 and the euro currency in 2002. However, its industry is one of the most fragmented and low-sized in the EU, with hardly any heavy industry and production. Its major income is from tourism, shipping, and agriculture. The core of its production is centered on small and medium-sized businesses, which are often family concerns. Foreign capital is still slow in coming, especially for productive use, due to its bureaucratic maze and corruption. For instance, the Hollywood blockbuster *Troy* was not filmed in Greece. Apparently this was due to the experiences of filming *Captain Corelli's Mandolin* in Cephalonia, which was plagued by inefficiency, to say the least. Economists are urging the necessity for improving conditions for domestic and foreign private-sector investment.

Bribes or Oiling the System?

A Greek-American friend who returned to his ancestral country runs a mechanical engineering company dependent on exports (a rare Greek initiative). He grew tired of having to continuously bribe officials inside public utility and energy companies to make things happen. Since bribery in Greek is called *ládoma* (literally, oiling), one day he turned up with two five-liter cans of olive oil from his village and handed them over, in effect highlighting his exasperation with the system. No one noticed the irony. He was thanked for his gift and everyone complimented his home village for producing one of the finest olive oils in the world. However, he is philosophical and a realist who understands the pros of working in Greece.

A key obstacle in the development of Greek industry and setting up businesses are the unions. They lack any sense of how market forces operate. In the city of Patras they were seen as directly responsible for the closure of the two main employers in the region, Pirelli and the textile factory Piraïki Patraïki. The workforce was made redundant and the trade union leaders continued with their Party careers.

But it is in merchant shipping that Greeks excel; they rank first in terms of tonnage, holding over 16 percent of world tonnage. Furthermore, they handle up to one-third of world shipping.

THE BUSINESS CULTURE

Greece offers a kaleidoscope of self-taught businessmen, and thousands of family enterprises, some of them going back several generations, each with its own way of doing things. This makes for widely varying business cultures. Therefore, when doing business with Greeks you will come across a wide range of characters, each with his or her own style, rules, and criteria.

However, since the mid 1990s most businesses began tuning in to the less colorful, "Western" ways. The mixture of skills and attitudes you will encounter will range from those of a shipowner who made it from being a ship's engineer, to British- and American-trained business postgraduates. There are also increasing numbers of Anglo-Greeks and American-Greeks who left their country of birth for the land of their forefathers, attracted by the new business climate.

TEAMWORK

Even those from a business culture where the occasional knife-in-the-back is considered a tonic probably also recognize the virtues of teamwork. Greece, however, is a place ill-adapted to teamwork, because too many people think they know better. And one thing they know better is that nothing raises alertness to its very peak than a good last-minute panic. For the uninitiated, this can be nerve-shattering. A sedative for your nerves when facing this situation is to maintain continuous communication throughout a project. Do this, even if your exchanges do not reflect what is actually happening on the ground. The point is to understand, perhaps to trust, your partners' *modus operandi*, and to be able to communicate to them any urgency you may feel is unforthcoming, and to locate any hiccups. How do the Greeks manage it? Remember that, if they are serious, their personal and professional life is well grounded within an extensive network of favors owed and *philótimo* by insiders and outsiders, to get things done. Your communication skill will enable you to share some of that personalized network because personal relations are very important. This does not mean that things can't go wrong.

Suspicion

One of the longest-running commercials on a Greek radio station features the traditionally suspicious Greek Cypriot man over in London looking for a real estate agent to sell his property. He bumps into a female compatriot who recommends the office in question in glowing terms, adding that they are "really honest kids." The man's immediate response is a suspicious, "Tell me, are these honest kids relatives of yours?" She answers "No," thereby advertising the fact that the agency's reputation transcends family connections.

All in all, you may feel you are walking up a steep mountain and want to give up halfway. Then something happens, as if people have decided they have given you the runaround for long enough and it is time to deliver. Something happens, and things fall into place.

Overall, Greek team members are talkative, gregarious people, and quick to take up opportunities.

MEETINGS AND NEGOTIATIONS

Agendas are often either nonexistent or produced at the very last moment, and then sidelined. Most people may have very pertinent opinions but are often reluctant to step forward and show initiative. The reason is that they believe decisions take place outside the meeting, no matter what is agreed on. This perception can act as an excuse for individuals changing aspects of the agenda. Considerable conversational overlapping can take place. Their mercurial minds also open up to new possibilities as negotiations develop. Imagine their brains, if you like, as a Web page with many hyperlinks leading to new ventures and ideas; while you are conversing with them on a specific issue, they are continuously clicking on those hyperlinks, giving you the feeling that you are "losing them" in a dozen different directions.

Greek negotiators know how to strike a deal and nothing makes them focus harder than if they believe there is a deal in it for them. They can be tough, fair, and remarkably imaginative; in other words, finding alternatives and shortcuts comes naturally to them and may surprise your sense of procedure and answerability.

One of the great pleasures of doing business in Greece, and one that makes you forget the frustrating moments, is that it has one of the world's greatest traditions of hospitality and entertainment. Expect successful business dealings to be accompanied by hospitality.

Plus Ça Change . . .

As far back as 1914 the Anglo-Greek author and businessman D. Cassavetti contrasted the Greek working ethos with German discipline, which, he noted, was "unsuited to the Greeks." The Greek, he observed, "is a man of resource and taught to think for himself." He understood that the chief characteristic of the Greek in Greece is that "he has not learned the habits of mental discipline, for he has never gone through the mill; life is too easy for him there, and so the iron does not enter the soul." Though this was written before the avalanche of disasters to befall the people, in many respects, his observation, on the business side, still holds true.

PRESENTATION AND LISTENING STYLES

Greeks are often suspicious. They wonder what's in it for *you* that you should be so willing to offer them something. They want to know what is in it for them. This can occasionally present you with a challenge in clinching a deal.

They enjoy concisely presented information and listen with attention as long as interest is held. They may ask questions at the end. They are easily bored with paperwork and their attention span is about forty-five minutes. However, there are occasions when their boss and his partner(s) may engage in lengthy speeches. If that is the case, you are advised to sit tight and let things take their course. Certainly, they will sit politely on until you finish your own presentation.

As mentioned earlier on, Greeks are inclined to be more expressive than concise. This means that, by your standards, they can take a long time to make the case in conversation, with much repetition of examples. It means that conveying information can be more time-consuming than you are used to.

Talking to a senior person, formality counts. So if he or she is the chairperson (whether of a small organization or a company) acknowledge their rank by using, even if you are speaking English, *Kýrie/Kyría Próedre* "Mr./Mrs. Chairperson."

LEADERSHIP AND DECISION MAKING

The bottom line is that decision making functions in a patriarchal system. But it is a system that thrives on improvising, delegation, and passing responsibility. You will often come across situations where everyone seems to know what needs to be done and how. For the outsider this can confuse things, but does not make them impossible. Take note that it is rare for clear instructions to be communicated. Verbal commitments are often not indicative of things to come.

MANAGING DISAGREEMENT

In case of disagreement it is essential to keep options and communication channels open and to avoid getting into entrenched positions. Greeks will try to find a solution around the disagreements. If government agencies are involved, then be prepared for stubbornness, bribery, petty posturing, and interminable bureaucracy.

ETIQUETTE

It is important to build the right sort of relationship in business and this is traditionally done over food and (moderate amounts of) drink. A Greek will want to invite you to his favorite restaurant. Your schedule should allow for this. It is as important as "pub socializing" is in the City of London. If you are apprehensive that such closeness leaves you exposed to making *faux pas*, relax. Greeks will make generous allowances for foreigners; mistakes of etiquette even endear foreigners to them. But lengthier interaction implies that etiquette rules and local sensibilities are gradually adhered to. Greeks rarely say "Thank you," but it is good for a foreigner to acknowledge the receipt of something with "*Efcharistó*" ("Thank you").

PUNCTUALITY

The lack of punctuality in Greece reflects the fact that not only did the Greeks invent the word "chaos," they seem to have incorporated it into their lives. Chaos is commonplace; there are no set rules, and things can change from day to day. You adapt by accepting it as a minor everyday inconvenience, which is more than compensated for by the advantages of the Greek lifestyle.

Your meeting partners will usually arrive from ten to forty-five minutes late. Make your appointments for the morning, before lunch if possible. Schedule two, maximum three, appointments a day if they are in different locations (especially in Athens). Cancellations and relaxed timekeeping are not unusual. Again, good personal skills enable you to make up lost time.

EYE CONTACT

Keep it steady. It is considered polite to maintain eye contact with your colleagues to show interest. Of course, if you come from a culture that stands stiff as a statue, eye contact can become a torturous affair. In cultures where body (and facial) language is more developed, eye contact is just one means of indicating personal attention.

CONTRACTS AND FULFILLMENT

Contracts are binding only when signed and sealed, though they can be skillfully reinterpreted. Greeks prefer them to be "impressionistic" rather than overprescriptive. They may also view a contract as a permanent final draft rather than as the last word and sacrosanct. Terms can be changed if the circumstances change, and even an American-style team of lawyers may have trouble pinning down the specifics.

One North American observed that in most parts of the world the wheels have to be greased, but in Greece they have to be greased more. She also noticed that even the "bribery landscape" is not fixed but changes according to circumstances. This means you are liable to experience extreme emotions in a very short time; one day you are flying high, the next you are chewing the carpet in despair, and by the afternoon you have liftoff again.

Do We Have A Deal?

Beware of words. During the buildup to the Athens 2004 Olympic Games, the International Olympic Committee visited the country in the belief that all relevant security purchases had been agreed to and signed. That was not the case. Indeed, an IOC official observed at the time that generally when someone tells them that something has been signed, they understand that the signatures are in place, the ink has dried, and money and goods will change hands. However, when the Greeks say that something has been "signed," they may simply be "announcing a deal." The Greek reality was that choices were still being made, especially since one of their main contractors was encountering major problems.

WOMEN IN BUSINESS

Women are increasingly active in the business world. As a woman, you will witness apparent sexism toward your female Greek colleagues, but do not underestimate their ability to hold their own ground. You will also encounter great courtesy and respect.

chapter nine

COMMUNICATING

MAIL

Envelope addresses written in the Latin alphabet are as sure to reach their destination as in those in the Greek. Greeks enjoy a polite form of expression and in correspondence prefer to use phrases like "Best regards" and "Yours truly," rather than a simple name sign off. Be formal, especially with elders, those in office, and of distinct higher rank.

TELEPHONE

Getting a line in Greece is quite easy. This is done by applying to OTE (the Hellenic Telephone Organization, but just ask for "OTEh"). Phone calls abroad are expensive but you can link up with some line providers that cut the cost all around. Connections are generally sound. There is still no cheap prepay card system.

Greece took to cell phones so quickly they never stood a chance of becoming a status symbol. Everybody has one.

Useful Numbers	
139	International call information (English, French, German)
131	Directory inquiries for OTE subscribers
11811	Yellow pages
171	Tourist police
1402	Wake-up call

THE INTERNET

There are Internet cafés all over Greece. Often you will see two or three people around one terminal—the Internet is not as solitary a pursuit as it is in other countries. There is ample provision for personal PCs; Greece is not an Apple country. A good search engine is www.google.com.gr. You can also try www.pathfinder.gr.

THE PRESS

In general, the media is the hands of four major press barons whose interests include construction companies dependent on lucrative state contracts. The national press is centered in Athens.

Readership figures are very low: just over 80 people out of 1,000 buy daily papers. Many more than that number read the front page since newspapers are fully displayed at most of the *períptero* (kiosks). Therefore, newspapers can act as informal daily posters (both proprietors and government are aware of this). Recently, the major newspapers have become heavy with glossy supplements. There are few Greek journalists outside Greece, and only a handful who are permanent staff. Greek reporting is heavily reliant on commentary.

TELEVISION

If television in the U.S.A. reflects the interests of corporate America and Britain's BBC the interests of the Oxbridge establishment, the development of Greek television was shaped by its dependence on the PASOK Party and its business partners. The first big owners came from the world of newspaper publishing; because of their media experience they were the obvious movers and shakers in the business. The medium really came into its own in the late 1980s with the licensing of commercial channels. Soon a hundred and forty broadcasters took to the air, many of them illegal. Eventually only four or five came to dominate the ratings. Another twenty operate on shoestring budgets. Their survival was made possible by the state turning a blind eye to their giant tax bills, and other benefits.

The state broadcaster, ERT, has three channels with many quality programs, especially ERT 3. The licensing fee is included in the electricity bill (irrespective of whether you have a receiver or not). News programs can last for two hours and contain little hard information. Most commercial ones should be classified as news entertainment shows, with an emphasis on sensational items accompanied by dramatic background music. Up to six windows at a time can appear on the screen carrying a debate where guests compete for speaking time. Some channels show up to twenty minutes of advertising an hour. It is fair to say that TV has killed the art of conversation in many households. Many areas outside Athens have poor reception quality, which is probably a blessing.

FOREIGN MEDIA
This is an interesting relationship. Greek society is more speculative than investigative, more likely to comment than to report. In the media this translates into a reluctance to follow stories through, question evidence, or instigate probing

questions. After all, this is a small society where media, government, and business interests often cross over; you never know whose shoes you may be stepping on—perhaps those of someone who will kick you out of your job. But stories printed in the foreign media are immediately on the record and can be safely referred to without incurring serious penalties. This means that the Greek media is almost obsessive about reports of the country in the foreign media. A particularly challenging article or documentary (especially if produced in the U.S.A. or Britain) can dominate the front pages for days.

SWEARING

You might as well read it here—after all, it is the bread and butter of Greek popular conversation. That word is *malaka*. If the stress falls on the last "a," *malaká*, it means "softly" or "gently," a wonderful word. If the stress falls on the second "a," *maláka*, it means a sort of rare soft cheese, and also "you stupid jerk-off." It is used regularly and carries no great force. Another word is *gamóto*. Ostensibly it means "f*** this," but often acts as an acceptable exclamative of exasperation or appreciation, as in "I am doing this for the glory of Greece, *gamóto!*" It is all a matter of contextualization; don't try experimenting with it.

Otherwise, Greeks are reluctant to swear, despite a highly sophisticated range of expressions, which, unlike those of the English language, are not limited to scatological and "orificial" references. In this respect, American and Afro-American English compete quite healthily with Greek. But as you would expect from a pious and family-loving nation, many insults involve various relatives and holy items in their construction, and can be quite oedipal too, with "mother" topping the list, while "father" is invariably absent. A favorite is *gamó to kandýli sou*, or "f***/damn your Holy oil lamp."

COURTESIES

The standard greeting is a handshake, both when you arrive and when you leave. If a meeting concludes in high spirits, then expect a stronger handshake and even some backslapping and shoulder shaking. Americans, Australians, Germans, and Yorkshiremen should feel quite comfortable with all this. Clinch the contract and there will be bearhugs all around. The lack of warm contact could signify that all was not well.

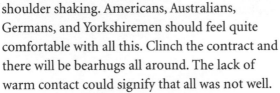

"Thank you" is an expression you will not hear too frequently. You will find yourself rendering some small service that the recipient will accept without batting an eyelid. That, for some reason, is normal, even though children are meticulously taught by their parents to say thank you, "*efcharistó.*"

BODY LANGUAGE

Greeks will often use their body language rather than words to communicate. Only the areas from above the chest are used to convey responses, opinions, or even make statements. Never show the palm of your hand with all fingers apart, as if you are indicating "take five." In Greece this means "excrement on your face," or that you are scum. It originates from Byzantine days when people used that gesture to rub soot on the face of criminals.

Greeks do not smile continuously during conversations, and neither is it an automatic social response—that is an American and British practice. They do smile in approval. If you smile continuously it can indicate that you are weak, simpleminded, lack seriousness, or are not paying attention.

CONCLUSION

The Greeks are a special people on a unique journey. They are heir to a multilayered heritage in a vital part of the world. They are generous, mercurial, emotional, instinctive, practical, and supreme improvisers. Personal interaction is vital to them. This means that life in Greece operates on many levels. Or rather, it operates on many crisscrossing levels, offering plenty of possibilities and a tremendous variety of lifestyles. The country embraces geographical variations one would associate with a small continent, only easily accessible. Socially, it has everything from the intensely private to the busy and cosmopolitan. The new generation understands its responsibilities, though not necessarily the challenges that lie ahead. Greeks live for the here and now, and this means they are ready to deal with just about anything, as it happens. The engaged visitor will emerge from the Greek experience enriched for life.

Appendix 1: Key Comparative Values

At the risk of oversimplification, here are some differences between the "Anglo-Saxon" world and Greece.

CORE VALUES AND CHARACTERISTICS

U.S.A., U.K.	Greece
U.S.A.: Personal initiative U.K.: Precedent	Family
U.S.A.: Doing it right U.K.: Caution/fair play	*Philótimo* (respect of personal duty above and beyond the law and personal grudges)
U.S.A.: Outgoing, self-advertising U.K.: Reserve	Suspicion
U.S.A.: Bottom line U.K.: Diplomacy and apparent compromise	Last-minute rush
Respect for law	Personal connections
U.S.A.: In your face U.K.: Self-effacement	Openness
Democracy	Love of debate
U.S.A.: Buddies U.K.: Polite estrangement	Friendships

CULTURAL FEARS

U.S.A., U.K.	Greece
U.S.A.: Being left behind U.K.: Straight talking, boasting	Turkish military threat
U.S.A.: Being disliked U.K.: Attacking underdogs	Powerful countries, especially America. Betrayal
U.S.A.: Being seen as a loser U.K.: Being overoptimistic	Taxes, bad health
U.S.A.: Being in an obviously un-American environment U.K.: Being taken over by Brussels, being seen as America's lapdog	Outsiders not understanding Greek particularities

MOTIVATION

U.S.A., U.K.	Greece
System/job	What can it do for me
Long term	Here and now, tomorrow may never come
Profit/doing it right	Money/so long as it works for the job at hand
Money/humor	Easy and secure life

STYLES OF COMMUNICATION

U.S.A., U.K.	Greece
Concise	Wordy, more explanations
Short memos, a little curt	More deferential, respectfulness is explicit
U.S.A.: Rather aggressive U.K.: Rather clannish	Could do with being more economic

culture smart! **Greece**

Appendix 2: The Greek Alphabet

Upper Case	Lower Case	Name	Pronunciation
Α	α	Alfa	a (as in *Athens*)
Β	β	Vita	v (as in *very*)
Γ	γ	Gamma	gh (soft, like a throaty "r")
Δ	δ	Delta	th (as in *the*)
Ε	ε	Epsilon	e (as in *egg*)
Ζ	ζ	Zita	z (as in *zest*)
Η	η	Ita	i (as in *sheep*)
Θ	θ	Thita	th (as in *bath*)
Ι	ι	Iota	y, i (as in *sheep*)
Κ	κ	Kappa	k (as in *can*)
Λ	λ	Lamda	l (as in *love*)
Μ	μ	Mi	m (as in *mother*)
Ν	ν	Ni	n (as in *no*)
Ξ	ξ	Ksi	x (as in *box*)
Ο	ο	Omikron	o (as in *dog*)
Π	π	Pi	p (as in *up*)
Ρ	ρ	Ro	r (as in *retsina*)
Σ	σ, ς*	Sigma	s (as in *sing*)
Τ	τ	Taf	t (as in *out*)
Υ	υ	Ipsilon	i (as in *sheep*)
Φ	φ	Fi	f (as in *friend*)
Χ	χ	Chi	ch (gutteral, as in *loch*)
Ψ	ψ	Psi	ps (as in *lips*)
Ω	ω	Omega	or (as in *bought*)

An accent on a vowel denotes stress.

*Used only at the end of a word

Further Reading

Guide Books

Gage, Nicholas. *Hellas: A Portrait of Greece*. New York: Villiard Books, 1987.

Hannigan, Des. *Lonely Planet Guide to Greece*. Melbourne, Oakland, London: Lonely Planet, 2004.

Kizilos, Katherine. *The Olive Grove—Travels in Greece*. Melbourne, Oakland, London: Lonely Planet Publications, 1997.

Leontis, Artemis (ed.). *Greece: A Traveler's Literary Companion*. San Francisco: Whereabouts Press, 1997.

History and Politics

Boatswain, T., and C. Nicholson. *A Traveller's History of Greece*. London: Weidenfeld & Nicolson, 2003.

Chalkokondyles, Laonikos. *Demonstrations of Histories*. (Originally, c. 1450.) Athens: Basilopoulos, 1996.

Fafalios, Maria, and Costas Hadjipateras. *Greece 1940–41 Eyewitnessed*. Athens: Efstathiadis, 1995.

Housepian Dobkin, Marjorie. *Smyrna 1922: The Destruction of a City*. New York: Newmark Press, 1998.

Koliopoulos, J. S., and T. M. Veremis. *Greece—the Modern Sequel, from 1831 to the Present*. London: Hurst, 2002.

Runciman, Steven. *The Fall of Constantinople*. Cambridge: CUP, 1990.

Thucydides, *The Peloponnesian Wars*. London: Penguin Classics, 1979.

Culture and Civilization

Beaton, Roderick. *George Seferis, Waiting for the Angel, a Biography*. New Haven, London: Yale University Press, 2003.

Cavafis, C. P. (translated by Keeley and Sherrard). *Selected Poems*. Princeton: Princeton University Press, 1992.

St. Clair, William. *Lord Elgin and the Marbles, the controversial history of the Parthenon sculptures*. Oxford: OUP, 1998.

Orthodox Tradition

Constantelos, D. J. *Understanding the Greek Orthodox Church*. Brookline, MA: Hellenic College Press, 1998.

Language

In-Flight Greek. New York: Living Language, 2001.

Biographical Novels

Tsirkas, Stratis. *Drifting Cities*. Athens: Kedros/London: Central Books, 1995.

Miller, Henry. *The Colossus of Marousi*. London: Norton, 1975.

Soteriou, Dido. *Farewell Anatolia: The Dead Are Waiting*. Athens: Kedros, 1996

Index

Acknowledgments

To my father, Spiros, for his patience; my late grandfather, Panos, for his knowledge; Marilena Mavroidi; Christos K. for his research skills; the Archdiocese of Thyateira and Great Britain; friends and family who forever respond with constructive comments; and the University of Westminster (Department of Diplomacy and Applied Languages) for its support.